"Burdens are lessened when we share.

More is accomplished when we work

together and have the opportunity

to be a blessing to each other.

It is good to belong."

Lynne Pearson

"The church's purpose is simple,

it is about loving God

and loving our neighbor.

When we listen for the needs in

our communities, and respond in a way

that brings good news for all, that is

how we really love our neighbor."

Rev. Kristin Joyner

Filling the Void

Voices From the None Zone

Compiled and Edited
by Rev. Kristin Joyner & Lynne Pearson

Contributors:

Bradley Beeman

Jan Bolerjack

Lara Bolger

Kelly Dahlman-Oeth

Meredith Dodd

Emma Donohew

Kristin Joyner

Joseph D. Kim

Kah-Jin Jeffrey Kuan

Rich Lang

Lynne Pearson

Jenny Smith

Jeremy Smith

Heather Sparkman

Dave Wright

Karen Yokota Love

Market
Square
BOOKS

Filling the Void

Voices From the None Zone

**Compiled and Edited
by Rev. Kristin Joyner & Lynne Pearson**

©2019 Rev. Kristin Joyner & Lynne Pearson
books@marketsquarebooks.com
P.O. Box 23664   Knoxville, Tennessee 37933

ISBN: 978-1-7323092-8-9

Library of Congress: 2019937250

Printed and Bound in the United States of America

* Except where noted, Scripture quotations are from the
New Revised Standard Version Bible, copyright © 1989 National
Council of the Churches of Christ in the United States of America.
Used by permission. All rights reserved worldwide.

Table of Contents

Foreword

Most would agree that church membership is on the decline. The United Methodist Church, to which I belong and in which the authors of this small volume are actively engaged in ministries, has been on a steady decline in membership in the United States since the 1960s, from a high of 11 million members to dipping below 7 million in 2016. Many people have been predicting the gradual death of the church in the United States which, if we're not careful, can become a self-fulling prophecy! As a leader in theological education and the president of a seminary that prepares leaders for the church, I have personally been rejecting such predictions.

The decline of church membership in the United States is a much more complex issue. While it is right and appropriate to question whether or not the ministries of the church continue to be relevant for this time and age, it is equally important to recognize the changing face of the United States. The changing demographics have made the United States a much more ethnically, culturally, and religiously pluralistic society than ever before. In addition, the explosion of urban centers has made life more economically complex and challenging with a concomitant impact on religious life and involvement. In spite of these realities, while the church is on the decline, it is far from dead!

The narratives of these clergy leaders in the most reli-

giously challenging region of the United States, the Pacific
Northwest, which is often referred to as the "None Zone," offer
testimonies and evidence of vibrant church life and ministries
that speak to the changing realities of 21st century society.
As Reverend **Rich Lang**, the District Superintendent of the
SeaTac Missional District, reminds us, the "None Zone" can
be an "Abundant Zone," and he is seeing "true abundance in
congregations that are learning to build relational partnerships with others who share their values."

The stories each of these pastors share are powerful.
Their experiences can become best practices for the revival
of religiosity and church life, not only in the "None Zone" of
the Pacific Northwest but also in other regions of the United
States.

Doing ministry in this "None Zone," Reverend **Joseph
Kim** writes about a congregation that is "not ashamed to do
church, to be church, to be people *gathered* in love and *sent* for
transformation." For Reverend Kim, such "doing life together"
is counter-cultural. His congregation is "not ashamed to challenge the values of our society, the values of our American,
capitalistic, consumeristic, dog-eat-dog, love is weak, and
vulnerability is bad society," and in the process challenge the
isolation and division that define the American society.

Likewise, Reverend **Kristin Joyner**, who also serves
this congregation, shares about her ministry "to bridge the
work in the community with the community of the church."
Addressing issues of human fragmentation and isolation in
an urban area with growing economic challenges for a lot of
people who are experiencing homelessness or who are living
from one paycheck to another, Reverend Joyner speaks of
the mercy work at the intersection of the church and the
community to address the serious housing crisis and related

economic issues of the people in the community.

A number of these clergy and their congregations are addressing the critical challenges of affordable housing and homelessness in their ministries. The strategic plan of Reverend **Lara Bolger**'s congregation puts "a high priority on partnering with the city and other nonprofit service organizations to address hunger and homelessness." In a society defined pretty much by fear, Reverend **Meredith Dodd** shares the experience of her local congregation being asked to host a homeless encampment in their parking lot.

The church had to confront fear and anger from neighbors as well as members of the congregation. Through the challenges of hosting the encampment and learning to extend transforming love, the congregation also learned "what it means for a human being to be vulnerable." Similarly, Reverend **Kelly Dahlman-Oeth** acknowledges that there is much fear of the unknown within his congregation, particularly with persons who are struggling with homelessness, addiction, and/or mental illness, in spite of the fact that this is a congregation with a vision and desire to provide housing and services to the most vulnerable.

Reverend **Jan Bolerjack** reminds us of the importance of allowing mission to spring from the needs of the community around them and to work closely with the city officials, police, and the school district to identify needs and develop responses to create goodness in their community. Stepping out of their fear, these congregations have seen transformation in their midst as they seek to faithfully live out their faith.

Such stories of life-transforming ministries are not confined to local church contexts. Reverend **Dave Wright**, for example, talks about the pluriform chaplaincy ministry he is engaged in on a college campus that has transformed "[his] identity and vocation, calling [him] out from ministry as a way of bringing people into a specific faith community, calling [him] in to a ministry of presence that disrupts expectations." Reverend **Bradley Beeman**'s church has a heart for mission and outreach. One such mission takes place 10,000 miles away in Thailand, where the church is building boarding houses for orphans. The church has provided the love, the finances, the support, the prayer, and the labor for this mission project, and in doing so, they are "sharing the love of God in the None Zone and throughout God's creation."

Reverend **Emma Donohew**'s ministry has taken place in pubs, breweries, and bars where she has facilitated a weekly Pub Theology conversation for the past six years, during which Christian witness is lived out in civil dialogue and compassionate listening over a beer. Taking advantage of a city that is home to sixty breweries, Reverend Donohew has engaged Christians, Atheists, Agnostics, and people of other faiths in conversations on "death and mortality, consumerism, reproductive rights, online dating, doubt, climate change, compassion fatigue, money, and more," framing these conversations within the lenses of spirituality and faith.

Finally, the ministries that these clergy are called into in the "None Zone" exemplify radical inclusivity, grace, and forgiveness. Reverend **Jenny Smith** speaks of the level of authenticity and sharing in her congregation as transformational where "God's Spirit sits at the center of this community and welcomes all kinds of mess and pain and truth." Out of this radical inclusivity, God has given this congregation a bold vision of birthing ten new expressions of church in the next thirty years.

The journey to turn that vision into reality has started with a lay person in the congregation who is planting the first new church. Reverend **Heather Sparkman** tells a story of extending grace and forgiveness to a petty thief who had broken into their church property and stolen their security cameras. When the young man's mother asked a trustee why we had showed such kindness to her son, she was told, "...we all make mistakes, and God hasn't finished with us yet."

I am deeply grateful for the ministries of my United Methodist colleagues in the "None Zone." May the experiences and the stories they share be a blessing to all!

Soli Deo gloria!

The Rev. Dr. Kah-Jin Jeffrey Kuan, Ph.D.
President and Professor of Hebrew Bible
Claremont School of Theology

INTRODUCTION

None Zone or Abundant Zone?

Here in the Pacific Northwest, and particularly here in the global mission field of Seattle, our context is both one of fear and hope, of scarcity and abundance, of confusion and clarity. We are the Christ canaries in a deep cultural mine that increasingly is void of the oxygen we need to stay alive. And yet, this same cultural mine, has different forms of life growing within it. The mine has different ways of not merely surviving but thriving and revealing the treasure of a better world that is possible. Here in the Pacific Northwest, the proclamation of the gospel and the presence of the church is both floundering and flourishing. It is a time of despair and a time of enthusiastic creativity. The church as we have known it appears to be in irreversible decline. And yet, there are testimonies, here and there, now and then, that surprising new life is rising. This little book will invite you into some of those testimonies, and some of those struggles as a church on the front lines of resurrection and faithfulness.

For my part as a district superintendent overseeing the ministries of fifty-four urban congregations, I see both enormous potential, absolute need, and also the frustration of congregations who cannot and often do not want to shift priorities and practices so as to be more present in their own neighborhoods. As Dickens wrote long ago, "It was the best of times. It was the worst of times."

I see the best of times and true abundance in congregations that are learning to build relational partnerships with others who share their values. I think of the congregation who sold their back property so that a low-income housing community could arise. Although providing low-income housing is a positive common good, where I see hope is that the congregation who sold their property desires to build friendship with their new back door neighbors.

I see hope in the congregation solidly located in a middle class setting but nevertheless had the courage to open their parking lot to car campers. Next, they opened their church building to become the car campers living room, and their kitchen to become a true community kitchen. They did these things for the deeper purpose of building friendship: "Christ in you the hope of glory!"

I see hope in those congregations who embrace relationship and solidarity with those who practice other faith expressions. In our current political climate of scapegoating others, I am strengthened through the witness of those congregations who build friendship with mosque and temple, with ashram and meditation centers.

The declining numbers of Christianity do not capture my attention as much as less than faithful practices of the people called Methodist. The whole movement began as a revival practice to get out of the church building and into the street, to get out of ceremonial ritual and into public witness. From the beginning we identified with the poor, the working class, criminals, the ne'er do well. From the beginning we Methodists valued Christ's new incarnation that we encounter through experience. From the beginning we practiced small group intimacy asking, "how is it with your soul," and committing funds to build a strong common good. From the beginning our personal piety was formed in union with our social holiness. Both then, and now, such an expression of Christ is needed. Within this book you will see how a people formed through Cross and Resurrection, continue their faithfulness in a cultural time when it is hard to hear the Word of God, but here and there, now and then, such grace bursts forth and everything is changed. We live for those moments with the active expectation that they are present if only we will look and see.

Rev. Rich Lang
District Superintendent
SeaTac Missional District

CHAPTER ONE

Among Us

By Rev. Lara Bolger

[20] *Once Jesus[a] was asked by the Pharisees when
the kingdom of God was coming, and he answered,
"The kingdom of God is not coming with things
that can be observed;* [21] *nor will they say, 'Look, here it is!' or
'There it is!' For, in fact, the kingdom of God is among you."*

- Luke 17:20-21 (NRSV)

One afternoon, a woman and her daughter came to the church office after hours. Our faith formation coordinator opened the door and they entered with bags of groceries and some stuffed animals. The woman said that they had encountered a homeless family in front of the grocery store where they were about to go shopping. Their hearts were moved by the family and they decided to buy some food and toys for them. But when they were finally done with their shopping and walked out of the store to share what they purchased, the family was nowhere in sight. They looked around and could not find them anywhere. They were both very disappointed.

Not knowing exactly what to do, the mother shared that's when she remembered us. They had driven by our church on a Wednesday night and seen our signs for our community meal. She said to our staff member, "I knew you were a church that helps people in need." This is what brought them to the church and to our door. After listening to their story, our staff member received the gifts they brought for the family and then relayed their story to the rest of us. As she told the story, I remembered what one of the women who leads our weekly meal ministry (Open Kitchen) said to me. Never refuse the donations of food and gifts people want to share. Because, it is just as important to receive the gift and affirm the generosity of people, as it is to give.

That the woman remembered our church is not an accident. Since 2014, this church has been guided by a strategic plan which placed a high priority on partnering with the city and other nonprofit service organizations to address hunger and homelessness. As a result, community members make up 80 percent of those who help to serve our meals, while the remaining 20 percent of our servers are church members.

We partner with the city and three other non-profits to provide emergency shelter for families in the winter and transitional housing for men. For the last three years, we have served lunches in the summer to youth from the elementary school across the street who are not getting lunches because school is out. This year we raised the money to pay a youth intern to help coordinate these efforts.

This church decided to live out their calling to:

- Love God, neighbor, and self;

- Serve the community and world;

- Grow in our faith.

When I overheard one of the church members who serves regularly at the weekly meal asked why he does what he does, he quoted the church's purpose as his own, "to love, serve, grow." And it doesn't stop there. This year, we started plan-

ning and talking about the next four years. Our faith formation coordinator turned to prayer. She gathered a small group,
inviting people who were new to the church as well as people
who've been around for a while.

Every Wednesday evening, they sit in silence and pray
together. They pray to God for the church, for me their pastor,
for the community, for our faith formation, and whatever
comes up. They pray for forty-five minutes in the chapel and
then they share what came up during their time of silence.
They listen to what the Spirit is saying to them. Knowing that
they are praying for me every week is a humbling experience.

We are in conversation about what it means to be a disciple
at this time in the life of the church. We are discussing how
we can help people connect with our purpose to Love, Serve,
Grow. An exciting part of this conversation is how we are
incorporating spiritual practices. Love, Serve, Grow has been
mostly used to understand ourselves organizationally and we
are now exploring how it can shape our individual spiritual
experience, providing us a way to deepen our walk with God.

Which leads me to the obscure scripture text I chose. Some
interpretations say "within" as opposed to "among." As much
as I would like this scripture to be about an individual believ-
er's experience, I'm not convinced Jesus would address the
Pharisees in that way.

Rather, I find it more compelling to follow the NRSV
version that places the kingdom of God among the plural you,
and among us. What I really get excited about with this text
is that Jesus is correcting the idea that there are observable
signs associated with God's coming kingdom.

The challenge to the Pharisees is the challenge for all of
us, to accept that the kingdom of God is present in the ministry of Jesus and that it is not a matter of seeing as much as

trusting. Since the word belief often leads us to think in terms of dogma or assent to a particular way of thinking, I prefer to use the word trust. Trust includes the emotional as well as the intellectual and gets to the heart of where Jesus is taking us. There is an immediacy about this text that calls us to the present moment, to open our eyes to see with eyes of faith, the reign of God that is among us. God's reign is found in Jesus' ministry. And in Luke Chapter 4, we know Jesus fulfilled the scripture and shared his mission with us in these words:

> [18] "The Spirit of the Lord is upon me,
>   because he has anointed me
>   to bring good news to the poor.
>   He has sent me to proclaim release to the captives
>   and recovery of sight to the blind,
>   to let the oppressed go free,
> [19] to proclaim the year of the Lord's favor."
>
> – Luke 4:18

We are called to follow Jesus in his ministry. Our struggle to do that is articulated in both the Pharisees and the disciples in this section in Luke. Like the Pharisees, we want to know when God is coming. And like the disciples in this chapter, we want our faith to increase. Jesus is challenging them, and us, to not worry about when or how much, but to pay attention to where we place our trust.

When we place our trust in our possessions and daily life preoccupations, such as when, where, and how much, we can easily shift our reliance on the temporal for security. But when we pay attention to who Jesus paid attention to, what he cared about, then we too can begin to trust and act for liberating people from oppression, healing our spiritual blindness, and releasing us from captivity. Jesus awakens us to a life in the present for a future that is yet to be. He invites us to trust who the Spirit of the Lord places in front of us, so that we can be ready to respond to and create God's reign of justice, love, compassion, and peace.

This brings me to the None Zone. I first heard about the None Zone in 2005 when I was serving as a chaplain at the University of Washington Medical School and Harborview Medical Center. I was living in Queen Anne and attending Queen Anne United Methodist Church. The pastor knew I was on the ordination track. I was invited to assist with Sunday worship as much as I wanted while preparing for ordination. It was an exciting time at this church as they were in the midst of renovating their building.

The first Sunday we arrived they were getting ready to take out the pews. The pastor at the time told me about the book he had just read about the None Zone as a way of understanding the religious landscape in the Pacific Northwest. And in the new design and renovation of the church there was definitely an eye toward what would appeal to the people who do not check the religion box but do check the spiritual one.

After my ordination I served in California before moving to the Pacific Northwest in 2008. I have served three churches and become more familiar with the spiritual abundance that is the Pacific Northwest and the fluid boundaries that exist as described in the book. I serve with the people who check both the religious box and the spiritual box and are trying to live a life of faith in the Pacific Northwest.

In my experience, even religious people in the Pacific Northwest identify themselves first as individuals. The institutional or organizational identity is held rather loosely. As a result, there is little security to be found in the institution or institutional life. Therefore, Jesus' words resonate well. Even those who come to church regularly don't find their meaning in the organizational life as much as they do in what the organization is doing or how the organization is helping the individual. God's presence seems discovered most when people are putting their faith and love to action, finding ways to meet the needs of the community. My current congregation has discussed how a shared purpose is found when people from all walks of life come together and faithfully create a world of kindness and compassion.

The mystery of how we discover God's presence among us compels me daily and now leads me back to where I started this story. I don't know why the woman and her daughter decided to buy something for the homeless family they saw outside the grocery store that day. I don't know anything about their religious convictions. Were they members of a church, mosque, synagogue, nothing? What do they believe? None of this was ever discussed.

I wonder if maybe the mother was having a teachable moment with her daughter, or maybe, vice versa. Does that matter at all? What matters is that one or both of them were moved with compassion to respond to a family in need. This impulse to help another landed them at our door and their generosity was received with gratitude as they explained why they were there and thanked us for being a place they knew they could go to. Not only that, they trusted us to get the items to people who needed it.

They trusted us, the religious organization in the None Zone, to be the ones who would care for the marginalized in our community. The Kingdom of God is among us.

Reverend Lara Bolger is pastor of Redmond UMC and lives in Bothell with her husband, Robert, and their dog, Annie. She loves to laugh, read, walk her dog, play volleyball, go to concerts, watch movies, and eat anything with chocolate. Lara loves the "Wesleyan way": personal spiritual experience of God expressed in acts of love and social justice.

She is excited by conversations that foster and nurture a more creative and peaceful planet. She studied at UC-Berkeley, Duquesne University, and Claremont School of Theology. Ordained as an Elder in 2009, she has served St. Mark's UMC in San Diego, CA, Bothell UMC in Bothell, WA, and Blaine Memorial UMC in Seattle, WA.

Further reading:

- Killen, Patricia O'Connell, and Mark Silk, eds. *Religion and Public Life in the Pacific Northwest: The None Zone.* Lanham, MD: AltaMira Press, 2004

Discussion Questions

Chapter 1: Among Us

By Rev. Lara Bolger

Where do you see "God's presence among us?"

Whom do you trust in your community to help others?

CHAPTER TWO
Riding the Tide
By Rev. Kristin Joyner

*[36] Which of these three, do you think, was a neighbor
to the man who fell into the hands of the robbers?" [37]
He said, "The one who showed him mercy."
Jesus said to him, "Go and do likewise."*

– Luke 10:36-37 (NRSV)

The tide of Amazon, Microsoft, Google, Facebook, and Starbucks rolled into the Seattle area over the past decade or two. This tide didn't stop at the city boundaries but seeped out to us as well, in the Northeast suburbs of the county. It is with hesitant acceptance that the people in our community are realizing the waves of residents, traffic, and development are not a ripple that will ebb and flow.

This wave flows only outwards and its effects are flooding people with emotions ranging from panic and loss to excitement and riches. The disparity between those who gained from this epic storm and those who have been displaced because of it, is a widening gap.

What used to be a steady, mostly Caucasian of European descent working class suburb proud of its hominess, history, and homogeneity, is swiftly becoming ethnically and economically diverse. Universities and biotech have moved into the community, as well as those who make the daily solo commute into Seattle. Transit, social services assistance, and housing options are a mirage for the average workforce employee. We hear about improved conditions coming, but they hover just beyond the horizon.

Housing prices have tripled in a very short time. Those privileged enough to have purchased a home by 2007 have benefited from the lack of housing in our region. A colleague of mine told me that she and her husband purchased their home in 2007 for $250,000 and could now list it at $800,000. For this young family, their unexpected financial security is a palpable relief. Unfortunately, the majority of people who work in our school district, coffee stands, retail shops, and restaurants can't afford to live here.

People experiencing homelessness or those who live one paycheck away from it are increasing. Landlords, able to increase rent by leaps and bounds are gaining financially while their renters pay more than 50 percent of their income for housing.

What does all this change mean for a community? People claim they no longer know their neighbors. Neighbors who haven't come face to face with homelessness before, now see people holding cardboard signs at grocery stores. People who have called this community home for years are now homeless in a desert of social assistance agencies.

City council members and city staffers are working diligently for their constituents but are burdened with the pace and funding of government. City council recently discussed our community as having "solastalgia," a state of coping when a person's built and natural environment changes rapidly. It's exhausting, it's trying, it's both positive and negative, and it's a period of feeling out of control.

When a community is experiencing growing pains,

economic pains, feeling fractured, even broken, where do the people turn for comfort? When people hurt, followers of Jesus know that comfort and grace can be found in Christianity and in the communities of believers that gather.

Local churches are called to be a place of grace and love for those seeking sanctuary and salvation from the ills of the world. But here, in the None Zone, people check the box "none" and "no thanks" to religion.

This region is known for our rain, our love for the outdoors, and our deep commitment to the environment. Our people are known for their love of independence and their care for the greater world. Non-profit agencies from other parts of the country move to the Seattle area because of our desire to participate in positive global transformation.[1] In 2014, two nearby cities ranked in the top ten of America's Most Generous Cities, with Seattle ranking number one.[2]

Volunteerism is a popular and well-regarded way to spend time in our area as seen in our rank of number eight in the nation by the Corporation for National and Community Service.[3] People here are good. God is working here and we are joining in the work that is the undercurrent of what God is already doing, the *Missio Dei*. However, it is not through any claimed religion that people are doing this, it is through their own experiences. People here tend to claim their spirituality

1. Press Release Distribution. "Mavuno Relocates USA Office to Impact Hub Seattle." January 13, 2017.

https://www.prlog.org/12615163-mavuno-relocates-usa-office-to-impact-hub-seattle.html

2. Couch, R. "These are the Most Generous Cities in America." Huffington Post. Updated December 7,2017.

https://www.huffingtonpost.com/2014/06/28/most-generous-city_n_5537781.html

3. Volunteering and Civic Life in America website. Seattle-Tacoma-Bellevue, WA. 2015

https://www.nationalservice.gov/vcla/city/seattle-tacoma-bellevue-wa

as their motivation, not their religion.

The Church has a long history of community building. Our traditions have always included bringing people together for common purpose. I feel the passion and excitement of the people in Acts when the Holy Spirit gathers the people from all nations together to hear the promises of God, and to share in a community where all people will know they are beloved. People are at their best when they can share their joy, their love, and their hopes with one another. Communities are strong when they can bear one another's burdens, grief, and sorrows.

At Bothell United Methodist Church, my call as a deacon is to bridge the work in the community with the community of the church. The tumultuousness of our region has created an opening for the United Methodist Church to be present for the people who live and work as our neighbors. As I participate in city-sponsored "Community Conversations,"

I listen to the concerns of local residents. I hear the fear, the disconnectedness, and the desire for connectedness. In planning commission and city council meetings, I hear the panic of mobile home park residents as properties are sold and rezoned for denser housing, displacing these economically strapped seniors, veterans, and disabled people.

God is at work here. In our community there are people pushing for social systemic change, volunteering their time and money in acts of mercy. People here desire deep community ties and are pleading with the cities to encourage festivals, facilities, and parks for gathering. We, the church, offer our buildings, our classrooms, our gardens, and our parking lots to join in as community-builders.

Over the course of a year, thousands of community members gather in Beloved Community as they come to Bothell United Methodist Church. We share our faith, our prayers, our radical hospitality, and extravagant generosity as we work towards mercy and justice for those who are suffering.

Each Sunday night at 5pm, volunteers at Bothell Community Kitchen prepare and serve a fresh, hot meal for members of our community. Many people who eat here have homes, apartments, and mobile homes, while some live in their cars or outside. We are neighbors, and all are welcome to serve or to eat here and experience our radical hospitality. Community resources, pamphlets for local support agencies, information about housing, and food stability is available. We have a process for helping people with groceries, gas, and showers.

Our congregation supports the North King County Winter Shelter by making and serving meals. Financial contributions support the operation of this low barrier shelter. Last year, thirty-four guests were able to access more stable housing by working with the case management that was offered at the shelter. For others, their conditions during the winter were improved by moving indoors during the cold and wet months. The shelter becomes a community experience for many of the patrons. They enter into pleasant conversation with people without fear or judgment.

Our mercy work includes helping mothers at New Ground Bothell in becoming established in their apartment. Volunteers work with the mothers by purchasing needed household items. For some of the mothers, these may be the first new items they have ever had. Other volunteers assist with cooking classes either in the kitchen, or by babysitting while the mothers are in the class. This work transforms the mothers' relationships with each other, our members, and their young families.

In the south end of King County, Riverton Park United Methodist is in a neighborhood with very high rates of poverty and homelessness. Workers from Bothell UMC partner with Riverton Park UMC in their work that is transforming their large property into various forms of transitional housing. People with different gifts and skills build, paint, and construct facilities that will give local people more stability. This transforms the conditions of the area, the lives and relationships of the neighbors, and the people who are doing the work.

Mercy work is important in helping people who are in difficult situations, or even in crisis. Mercy work brings dignity and honor to all of God's people, especially when they are hurting. In addition to mercy work, we must work to make systems and structures that balance the needs in a community and reach a place that is fair for all.

Bothell UMC has representatives that are working for justice as our region is experiencing a housing crisis. Housing is only available to people who can provide a profit. Until we have housing available for those who cannot provide a profit, only people who can provide a profit will get housing.[4] If this continues, our housing conditions will worsen.

As part of the Kenmore Bothell Interfaith Group, and organized by the Church Council of Greater Seattle, members of Bothell UMC are working with partners to advocate for affordable housing justice. This group is meeting with members of the Regional Taskforce on Affordable Housing.

This work brings together faith communities that share their values and policy recommendations for housing in King County. The goal is to encourage more availability of housing for low income people. In addition, we are present at local city council and planning commission meetings to witness to our desire for fair housing strategies for the low-income residents

---

4 Credit given to Tim Harris, founder of Real Change Newsletter. http://realchangenews.org/users/timothy-harris

in our local cities.

While our efforts are not perfect, and won't solve the housing crisis alone, we are working with partners as we strive to live out our purpose of Becoming Christ in the Community. Christ in the community means that all will know they are valued and loved and a part of the Beloved Community of God. We not only walk alongside those who are suffering, we, too, are experiencing what they are experiencing and working for solutions. We are riding the tide with our neighbors, loving them as Christ loved us.

While riding this tide, we are evangelizing. Although, that "e" word is not used here very often. In order that it won't be misconstrued, let me explain that word to mean that we want to share with the world what we understand to be good news for all. Good news isn't good news if it isn't good news for everyone. Evangelism is intended to be a sharing practice, not a converting practice. This isn't a culture of telling other people what to believe or how to believe it. It is a culture of being present in all the places in our communities, of intently listening, and of responding with care. When we do this with a deep rootedness in our faith and alongside our trust in God, our responses are directed by the Creative Creator, not our pocketbooks or egos.

The United Methodist Church proclaims, "Open Hearts, Open Minds and Open Doors." It is those open doors that we are paying attention to. Inviting people in is an important practice, but disciples go out those doors into the world to find more of God each day. Fixing the church programs to attract people into the doors *may be* worthwhile, but going into the world to be church is *definitely* worthwhile. This is where we put into practice what we believe to be the grace and love of God. It is where we experience relationships that expose us to the width and breadth of all that is created in God's image.

The tide is rising. Increasing development, density, shifting economies, flowing migration, gaps of connectedness, harsh divisiveness, all of these things are happening around us. Some people dismiss the church's relevance, and think it is disappearing like words in the sand. Words carved in the sand remain until the tide flows over them, changing the formation of the sand. But the sand is still there, waiting to be shaped again. The tide doesn't ever stop, it continually changes the shape of the sand. When we go out into the world and dive into the voids, we too are being reshaped.

The church's purpose is simple, it is about loving God and loving our neighbor. But we can make it very complex and our work can be misinterpreted and full of flotsam and jetsam. This book project was inspired to clarify who we are and how we practice who we are, and how we bring that into the world. We know that when we listen for the needs in our communities, and respond in a way that brings good news for all, that is how we really love our neighbor. The tide is a constant motion, and while it is rising, so too will the church. We aren't running from the waves, we are riding this tide filling the voids with life giving water.

Rev. Kristin Joyner holds a Master of Arts in Ministry, Leadership, and Service from Claremont School of Theology and serves as a deacon at Bothell United Methodist Church. She is passionate about letting the local community know that the church is a place where all are welcome and to empower disciples to be active in service alongside those who have the greatest needs.

Kristin understands networking and connecting people locally and globally as the way to experience God's Beloved Community and is the way toward true peace and justice.

Discussion Questions

Chapter 2: Riding the Tide
By Rev. Kristin Joyner

What happens when churches work with community groups?

When should a church be involved with politics?

CHAPTER THREE

Called Out...
and Called In

By Rev. Dave Wright

*I know your works; you are neither cold nor hot. I wish that you
were either cold or hot. So, because you are lukewarm, and
neither cold nor hot, I am about to spit you out of my mouth.*

-Revelation 3:15-16 (NRSV)

It Has to Start Somewhere

It was a brilliantly blue summer day in the Pacific Northwest. The University of Puget Sound, a United Methodist-related liberal arts college with independent governance and a
very secular campus culture, shone as a green, park-like gem
nestled in the residential neighborhood of North End Tacoma.
Puget Sound was also my home as an undergraduate student,
ten years earlier.

I was returning to start my role as university chaplain and
director for Spiritual Life and Civic Engagement, following in
the footsteps of my friend and mentor, Jim Davis. As I write
this, twelve years later, I realize now how little I knew about
the ministry I was beginning, and how little I knew about how
it would change my life.

This seems ironic, in hindsight. When I was a student at
Puget Sound, I was deeply involved in religious life there. As a
young adult, the chaplaincy at Puget Sound was a remarkable

laboratory for my own emerging commitments to a ministry that was rooted in the social gospel and liberation theology while still attending to relational and spiritual interpersonal needs. My time as a student involved an ecumenical, inter-faith-friendly, United Methodist-led chaplaincy, which was tremendously important in equipping me as a leader, a pastor, and a human.

As I assumed the role of university chaplain, the charge presented to me (in various ways) by my bishop, my dean, my advisory committee, and other chaplains was essentially this: I was there to serve all students, to be present to all members of the campus community.

This invited me to dive into the wild diversity (and apathy, and antipathy) of all the ways the people I was appointed to serve might connect with or have little use for my identity as United Methodist clergy or more broadly as a Christian leader.

One of the first surprises that helped me to begin breaking down my assumptions about what chaplaincy in higher educa-tion encompassed took place in my first week back on campus. Due to some staffing changes, I was asked to be a part of our suicide prevention efforts at Puget Sound.

While I could draw on my early training as a hospital chaplain to engage in this critical effort, this non-religious, institutional need helped me understand my work as part of the institution, and as part of our sweeping commitment to support community members struggling with issues of mean-ing and existence.

As I stepped into this role, I found myself increasingly working to integrate intercultural and interfaith efforts, and chaplaincy became disassociated from "belief" to instead dealing with questions of identity and belonging. My roots in liberation theology connected with my emerging post-liberal commitments to inclusion and equity to transform my ministry, emphasizing the ways I could journey with historically minoritized bodies and voices in higher education – a context designed for white, Christian, male, and affluent bodies and voices.

In this new world, I found myself having to live in the tension between expectations. Church colleagues assumed it was a cushy life, playing with college students and maybe occasionally offering some support to a homesick student. Colleagues in higher education often initially approached me cautiously, expecting me to be a pious thumper of bibles, or a clone of my predecessor, or someone who was there to serve a niche market of "spiritual" students.

Within my own identity as a Christian, my role challenged me to interrogate my own theology and practice to make space for those who are not Christian, deepening my commitment to engage non-Christians as full, equal, and vital partners both in campus and cultural conversations about inclusion, identity, and resources – rather than as afterthoughts of a culturally Christian-dominant church.

This early rhythm of conflict and questioning drew me into a fundamental questioning of the charge I had been given by so many: what did it mean to be engaged in a ministry of presence and support for ALL members of my community?

Searching for Language and Meaning

As I settled into my position at Puget Sound, one of my struggles was to find a way to frame the wild creativity I encountered in the social/spiritual lives of my students. Older tropes like "Spiritual but not religious" were dismissed. Sociological and demographic research constructed the identity of being religiously "None," but most of the "Nones" I knew were deeply engaged with systems of meaning – they might have checked "None" on a survey, but didn't live with an absence of spirituality. Some might have closely adhered to a specific faith tradition or denomination, others were deeply anti-religious, but most were...something else.

A few years into my chaplaincy at Puget Sound, I first encountered the term "pluriform" in the work of Rhonda Hustedt-Jacobsen and Jake Jacobsen. Loosely put, in their work "pluriform" pointed to the ways in which many college students constructed spirituality that was shaped by individual and cultural appropriations of various religious, spiritual, and cultural practices.

This personal, contextual construction of religion and spirituality often was more present, more real, more tangible than the specific traditions or forms most of us recognize – Jewish, Christian, Muslim, Buddhist, Baha'i, and so on. Students might carry these traditional labels, based on family, culture, or choice, but their own worlds were shaped by exploration and creation of spiritual identity, rather than repetition or regurgitation of static models of belief.

Since that time, I have been haunted by the power and concept of pluriform religious life, and have sought to weave it into the construction of my chaplaincy. This is not to reduce religion or spirituality to a random amalgam of nice ideas, or a generic least common denominator, but rather describes the ways in which individuals create, grow, and evolve their own spiritual practices and beliefs in a pluralistic world. While such practice must attend to the risks and challenges that appropriation poses, I have come to believe that the best way that I can understand my ministry has been as part of the evolution and development of a pluriform chaplaincy in higher education.

Making it Happen

As I have come to identify with this concept of pluriform chaplaincy, I continue to emphatically retain my identity as a United Methodist Christian clergyperson. This begs the question: what does "Christian ministry" look like in this milieu? How do I embody my denominational call to "make disciples for Jesus Christ" in a ministry role where that effort (as often expressed) is antithetical to pluriform chaplaincy and the purpose of the community I serve? I offer the following snapshots as a glimpse into the ongoing work of pluriform chaplaincy rooted in, but not focused on, my own faith tradition and identity.

- **Re-framing the "Peer Ministry" program** I inherited as an "Interfaith Coordinator" program, using a simple language change to better include and welcome students from various backgrounds into campus religious and spiritual leadership.

- **Continuing traditions that serve Christian students,** including an annual Festival of Lessons & Carols, Easter services, and more – while also becoming heavily involved with the annual Campus Passover Seder, Eid banquets, and similar traditions of other faith communities.

- **Working to develop an integrated campus center** that engages a wide range of identities – related to race, gender, sexuality, religion, and more – and how we show up in the larger world.

- **Helping to develop a "Logger Language Liaison" program** in which students who are fluent in languages other than English are available to help welcome and support the families of new students whose home language is not English – freeing new students to fully engage the campus while returning students support those families.

- **Connecting students with a range of campus and community resources** to address needs from food insecurity to registration problems to relational violence – and everything else.

- **Building campus and civic solidarity** with a Vietnamese Buddhist Temple after the Temple is targeted by hateful Christians. Bringing student volunteers to help clean up vandalism at the Temple and build relationship with Temple leadership.

- **Managing the administrative side of our institutional suicide prevention program**, freeing our clinical psychology staff to work with students about their needs rather than having to handle as much paperwork and policy.

- **Supporting student-led, student-initiated clubs and communities** that serve Christian, Jewish, Buddhist, Pagan, Baha'i, Hindu, Muslim, and other faith-related populations.

- **Advocating for appropriate institutional inclusion** of resources for those from minoritized religions and cultures (honoring holidays, dietary requirements, and more).

- **Organizing a multi-faith panel on race and religion** as part of a national conference on Race and Pedagogy hosted at Puget Sound.

- **Creating pluriform spaces for gatherings to celebrate lives that we have lost,** trying to honor both the identities of the deceased and the breadth of identities within the campus community.

- **Advocating for inclusion and accommodation** for those whose holidays, faiths, and festivals don't align with dominant Christian-cultured realities.

These are just some examples of what ministry looks like in my context, emphasizing the need to continually work to try to understand and engage with the evolving nature of our campus and our broader culture. They represent some of the ways in which pluriform chaplaincy has less to do with traditional patterns of pastoral care, worship, and faith-community leadership (although at times I get to do all those things, too) and rather is about working to make space for the fuller inclusion of all those who are part of our campus.

Claiming Pluriform Chaplaincy

Chaplaincy continues to transform my identity and vocation, calling me out from ministry as a way of bringing people into a specific faith community, calling me in to a ministry of presence that disrupts expectations, what I've been calling pluriform chaplaincy. Early in my chaplaincy career, working in hospitals in North Carolina, I found myself repeatedly in ministry with folks who were surprised that someone with my personal appearance, beliefs, lifestyle, and more could be a pastor.

I began living into the awareness that by not meeting certain social expectations, some people could connect with me who would not otherwise want to engage with religion or spirituality. Others found that encountering a pastor who didn't embody their stereotypes of what a clergyperson should be allowed us to drop some pretense and social nicety and be more honestly present to one another. While there were always some who shut me out, over the course of those early years, I found a unique sense of vocation in making use of my own identities to challenge others' expectations, opening new paths to engaging with a wider range of people than might typically be willing to connect with a religious professional.

This seed from early in my career, the idea that breaking assumptions can be an important form of ministry, has grown in me for almost twenty years, feeding a belief that in an age of secularism and stereotyping about religion I am best able to express the love of a radically gracious and inclusive God through a life of action that makes space for all people to be included in the beloved community. I increasingly believe that the best way to serve and follow Jesus is to let go of our obsession with getting other people to serve and follow Jesus.

- I cannot obsess with making other Methodists. We're cool, but not that cool. Instead, I wonder what we can do to help support and develop fellow humans who take caring for other people, and caring for God's creation, seriously?

- I cannot obsess with making other Christians. Trying to convert others is the best way to ensure they run the other direction. How can I live in a way that suggests that following Jesus is not about dominance or erasing who you are, but that it is about celebrating who you are and experiencing LOVE in your life?

- I cannot obsess with making people think about "religion." Religion too often poisons our world. How can I journey with people to find meaning, to make sense, to experience hope, grace, love, joy, and redemption in a world where matters of meaning are too often secondary to matters of power and profit?

I could go on, but the concept of disruption infuses my ministry. I follow one who did not meet the expectations of his

36

culture, his calling, his faith. I own that, and while I am not
the One I seek to follow, in others' footsteps what I have found
in chaplaincy in higher education is the potential to disrupt
the systems of dominance and power that have too often
defined Christianity in the United States.

Disruption in Practice

My involvement in what I frame as disruptive, stereo-
type-cracking ministry has often come in the form of my willingness to respond to the invitation of students, faculty, staff,
and alum that are part of the community I serve. While there
are moments that I step forward on my own, the heart of my
work builds on relationships that trust me enough to ask me to
participate in things that might seem outside the line of what
is expected of a Christian clergyperson in this context.

One of the most formative moments took place in my first
years at Puget Sound. This nation was in the midst of its
tremendous struggles around Islam and Islamophobia in the
wake of the attacks of 9-11-01. A small group of students and
faculty cautiously approached me to see if I would be willing to
take on a key role in a public protest that was being planned.
Specifically, I was asked if I would be willing to preside over
a parodic funeral for the Right of Habeas Corpus, calling out
the Bush administration for its suspension of basic due process
for those being detained in terrorism of the "war on terror."
I agreed and participated in a gathering that featured a full
funeral procession through the student union, ending amidst
a row of trees first planted by Japanese-American students
prior to their removal to illegal imprisonment by the U.S.
Government in 1942, offering a homily on the "Death of Habeas
Corpus." Student artists attempted to distract the audience
from what was going on. In addition to the ways this ministry
has built bridges with students and colleagues who otherwise

had no connection to chaplaincy, the conversations and interactions that flowed from the event gave me space to begin reframing my understanding and practice of chaplaincy for the college.

Flashing forward a few years, I find myself in the midst of a very different disruption. As cultural trajectories evolve in our world and at Puget Sound, the last couple of years have seen a significant expansion of the need for individual spiritual and social care as a part of my work. With the natural limits of time and space still in play, new needs for disruption have emerged. In working to reinstitute better resources and growth opportunities for our larger student communities (those from Jewish and Christian backgrounds), I have had to entrust some of the activist work to other colleagues. Focusing on student needs has turned a portion of my chaplaincy from external campus partnerships to working with close colleagues to develop tangible resources to address student hunger. This commitment to disruption, to shifting and challenging assumptions and experiences of what is "normal" for the sake of what is needed, is ongoing and evolving, and requires that I continue to interrogate not only my own privileges and presumptions but the nature and efficacy of my chaplaincy. As with the Habeas Corpus protest, I am building bridges with other students and colleagues who might not have connected with religious and spiritual life on campus, and am again working to define and redefine the nature of chaplaincy at Puget Sound.

Closing Thoughts

The concept of disruption as ministry may feel challenging. I am comfortable with that. It challenges me every day I step onto our campus, and in all the ways I try to nurture my own identity as a Christian and as a United Methodist following the way of Jesus. At the same time, I would not trade it for

the world. This ministry has made me a better United Methodist, a better Christian, and a better human. Through it, God
is still at work in my bones, my fiber, and my heart. This experience is a gift that I would not trade. This is my vocation, my
calling, my ministry. For this, above all, I am grateful.

Citations and Further Reading

- Forster-Smith, Lucy (editor), College and University Chaplaincy in the 21st Century: *A Multifaith Look at the Practice of Ministry on Campuses Across America*. Nashville:
  Skylight Paths, 2013.

- Jacobsen, Douglas, and Rhonda Hustedt-Jacobsen *No
  Longer Invisible: Religion in University Education*. New
  York: Oxford University Press, 2012.

- Patel, Eboo, *Acts of Faith: The Story of an American
  Muslim, in the Struggle for the Soul of a Generation*.
  Boston: Beacon Press, 2007.

Rev. Dave Wright (him/they) serves as the university chaplain and
Director for Spiritual Life and Civic Engagement at the University of Puget
Sound, an historically Methodist-related liberal arts college in Tacoma,
Washington. Having previously served as associate pastor at Bothell
United Methodist Church, Dave's position at Puget Sound is in service to
the breadth of the university — students, faculty, and staff of all faiths and
no faiths and everywhere in between.

As a co-director of the Center for Intercultural and Civic Engagement, his work focuses on minoritized and historically underrepresented
communities on campus, and on building bridges and connections
between campus and the local community that foster the common good
for ALL people. Dave serves on the board of directors at Tacoma Community House, a church-related agency serving immigrants, refugees, and
asylum seekers, and is also the Peace with Justice Coordinator for the
Pacific Northwest Conference.

He is a former board member of the National Association of College
and University Chaplains, the past-president of the Association for
College and University Religious Affairs, and currently on the board for the
International Association for Chaplaincy in Higher Education. Dave was

also awarded NASPA's 2018 national Spirituality and Religion in Higher Education Outstanding Professional Award.   Dave's training includes a BA in Religion from the University of Puget Sound, an MDiv from the Divinity School at Duke University, and two years of CPE Residency at the University of North Carolina Hospitals.

In his down time, Dave enjoys traveling with his partner, spending time with his twin tabbies (The Beasties), cooking, and hiking. He also, in everyone's opinion, spends too much time on Facebook.

Discussion Questions

Chapter 3: Called Out and Called In
By Rev. Dave Wright

How can being in community with people of other faiths strengthen your own faith?

We live in a diverse world. How does this benefit or challenge you?

CHAPTER FOUR

Grace Interrupted
Rev. Heather Sparkman

[10] You are my witnesses, says the Lord,
and my servant whom I have chosen,
so that you may know and believe me
and understand that I am he.
Before me no god was formed,
nor shall there be any after me.

– Isaiah 43:10 (NRSV)

[8] In that region there were shepherds living in the fields, keeping watch over their flock by night. [9] Then an angel of the Lord stood before them, and the glory of the Lord shone around them, and they were terrified. [10] But the angel said to them, "Do not be afraid; for see—I am bringing you good news of great joy for all the people: [11] to you is born this day in the city of David a Savior, who is the Messiah, the Lord. [12] This will be a sign for you: you will find a child wrapped in bands of cloth and lying in a manger." [13] And suddenly there was with the angel a multitude of the heavenly host, praising God and saying,

[14] "Glory to God in the highest heaven,
and on earth peace among those whom he favors!"

[15] When the angels had left them and gone into heaven, the shepherds said to one another, "Let us go now to Bethlehem and see this thing that has taken place, which the Lord has made known to us." [16] So they went with haste and found Mary and Joseph, and the child lying in the manger. [17] When they saw this, they made known what had been told them about this child; [18] and all who heard it were amazed at what the shepherds told them. [19] But Mary treasured all these words and pondered them in her heart. [20] The shepherds returned, glorifying and praising God for all they had heard and seen, as it had been told them.

– Luke 2:8-20 (NRSV)

The season leading up to Christmas, also known as Advent, is a time of preparation. We prepare our hearts to celebrate the birth of the baby Jesus and to receive God's love anew. There is a song we sing in church during this time of preparation with these words as the chorus, "Love came down at Christmas, Love all lovely Love divine. Love was born at Christmas, star and angel gave the sign."[5]

While the beauty of the season never fails, in my house, this is also known as the season of stress. It's not that we don't anticipate the birth of Jesus. We do. Christmas Eve is my favorite church celebration of the year. But any pastor will tell you that Advent is a holy season of busyness in the church world and in our family the stress is double because we have two children with December birthdays.

Even in the midst of this chaos, grace creeps in and prepares us for the love of God that enters the world through Jesus. Each year, Christmas is a remembering of that love and a receiving of it once again.

Most years, I long for uneventful Advent seasons where the story of God is celebrated and felt, but also unfolds according to schedule with no surprises. One Advent season in particular my plans for a scheduled, orderly Christmas season were interrupted by grace moments and signs of God's love. In my years as a pastor I have learned that God rarely works according to human plans and schedules. Instead, grace erupts in unexpected moments and, like the first Christmas where God broke into human history through Jesus, life is never the same afterwards.

That year the church's Christmas play was more like *The Best Christmas Pageant Ever* than a polished Broadway

---

5 Rosetti, Christina. "Love Came Down at Christmas." *The United Methodist Hymnal: Book of United Methodist Worship*. Nashville, Tenn.: United Methodist Pub. House, 1989. Page 242.

production, but the story was lived as well as told. The young actor, who screamed at the director during rehearsals, refusing to sing in front of the small gathered crowd, found the voice of an angel and brought the packed church sanctuary to tears on performance night.

For weeks I watched as the director of the play coaxed, encouraged, and loved this young actor. She came from rough places, bouncing from home to home as a foster child before landing with a family that claimed her as their own and began the process of healing. The mending of wounds does not happen overnight, and the director of the play came along and added balm to the pain and fear that performing in front of others drew out in this child. Rehearsals ran long; anxieties were high about performance night. The stress level surrounding the play was at an all-time high.

But then, the grace crept in and the young girl found her voice and her confidence and believed in herself as a beloved child of God. Her voice proclaimed the beauty of the Christmas story not only in its melody but also in the very presence of the young woman up on the stage.

Love came down at Christmas, love all lovely, love divine. The power of that love can transform, and it did for that young actor. The director's love, a sign of God's love, transformed that sad and angry girl into a star. Her shining light on the night of the performance was a reminder to us all, of the God that sees our beauty within and loves us dearly. God wasn't done with stars and signs that Advent season.

As the big Christmas Eve celebration drew near, a knock came at the back door of the church, just two days before Christmas Eve and the afternoon of my son's birthday. I was ready to leave for the day and go home to celebrate with my son. Everything was ready for Christmas Eve service and I had worked long hours that week to finalize bulletins, plan hymns, and write a sermon. The knock was an unwanted intrusion on my plans to spend the evening with my family and delight in my son's birthday.

As soon as I answered the knock on the door and peered out into the misty, gray Washington afternoon I saw trouble standing there, waiting for me. Nickleby was known around town for his petty theft and other crimes. There were rumors that he was involved in a murder, but no one could ever prove this, and the police left him alone on that charge.

He was a tall man, well over six feet, dressed in a black hoodie and jeans. Slightly hunched over, whether from the cold or his own sense of defeat, I'm not sure.

He kept looking over his shoulder and shifting his weight from foot to foot, nervous and intimidating all at once. "I need to talk to you," he mumbled. I was not alone in the building, so I felt safe in inviting him to come in out of the cold.

"Nah. Can't do it." He looked over his shoulder again.

"It's only me and another pastor here. You're safe. I promise." He wasn't immediately convinced.

He hesitated, not ready to enter. He danced from foot to foot some more and looked up at me with unsure eyes. I nodded encouragement.

With one more glance behind him, he stepped through the door I held open and let it close behind him with a thud.

"My mom says I have to come talk to you or she is goin' to kick me out," he said.

He let that sentence hang in the air. As the moments ticked by and he didn't speak again I wondered if that was all he was going to say.

44

"Yes?" I prompted.

He took a deep breath, exhaled, and started to speak. Then, he stopped and looked over his shoulder again.

"You goin' to call the cops?" he asked.

"Um, I wasn't planning on it?" I said it more like a question than a statement, wondering where this was leading.

"I gotta tell you something but I don't want the cops comin'," he went on.

"How about this?" I asked. "I won't call the cops without letting you know first. Then, you can decide what you want to do."

We stood in the church playroom, among the small chairs and low tables used for Sunday school. The walls were painted a bright yellow and aqua. Cardboard cutouts about Jesus loving the little children and teaching people to share bread and fish decorated the walls. Nickleby looked about as out of place in that church playroom as the shepherds must have felt in the presence of the angels announcing the good news of the birth of Jesus so many years ago.

But like the shepherds, he must have felt some touch of Divine presence, a hint of God's grace because he said, "Ok. I trust you for now."

I exhaled, not even realizing I had been holding my breath. He towered over me, his height making my five-foot-five frame feel tiny in comparison.

"Let's go into the library and sit down. Can I get you coffee or tea?"

"Nah. Just some water would be fine."

I showed him to the library and went to get the water. When I returned he had positioned himself so he could see out the library windows. He nodded towards them, "So I can see if the cops come."

"Ok." I said. "I understand. Now, you wanted to talk to me?"

"You missing some security cameras?" he asked. Yes, we were. For the past three months we had been losing security cameras, about one every two weeks. The footage from the cameras showed a person reaching up, head covered in a hood pulled close and tight so that no facial features were visible, plucking the camera right off the wall. They were located up under the eaves of the church and we suspected someone tall had been stealing them. In truth, we had suspected it was Nickleby all along.

"I took 'em," he said. "Mom says I have to come clean before Christmas or she is kickin' me out and I don't got nowhere else to go."

A forced confession but one that took courage and some trust.

"Okay." I said, unsurprised by the news but relieved that this might end the repeated thefts of our cameras. "I forgive you."

This was not what he was expecting. I could see it on his face as he looked at me like I had just spoken in another language.

"Why would you do that?" he asked. It came out almost as an accusation.

By this point, the other pastor in the building, Golden, had come in the room. Nickleby knew Golden from around town and didn't seem to mind his presence.

"Because that's what God does for us," Golden stated simply.

Grace, undeserved love, affection, and good will. It is

46

just too much for us to comprehend sometimes. Answering misdeeds, with acceptance, doesn't match any system of human justice.

"I can't get 'em back," he said as if this might change the status of his forgiveness. This news didn't surprise Golden or me. We had seen them being ripped from the wall on the footage and knew that they wouldn't be any good even if they were retrievable.

"Sold 'em. Didn't even get much money for 'em and I needed that money to pay off a bad man who is after me for a debt. Sorry I took 'em but I didn't have any other choice."

It wasn't much of a confession, or apology, but that didn't matter. He was owning up to his trespass against us and the forgiveness was free for the taking. I watched his face as we reiterated our forgiveness and reassured him that grace was never earned or deserved but given as a gift.

I thought of those shepherds again, hearing about the birth of a baby that was God's love come down to earth and how fantastic and unbelievable that news must have seemed. Nickleby was receiving the same good news, just as the shepherds had and finding it just as fantastical and beyond belief as they had.

"Do not be afraid," the angels said to the shepherds. "Do not be afraid," we said to the man sitting before us.

"I bring good news of great joy," the angels said. "We can offer you forgiveness because God has forgiven us," we said. And we all inhaled the grace that was present with us in that room.

"What about the cops?" he finally asked, coming back to the practical consequences of his actions.

"Well, I won't call them without talking to you first. God

forgives us, but we still have to answer for our actions. Let me call the head of our trustees, the people who take care of the church property, and we'll work out a plan. Is that okay?" I said.

"Guess so."

When Gene, the trustees' representative, arrived, we sat and talked about options. Nickleby told us the trouble he was in with the man who was after him, and cried about how scared he was for his life. We encouraged him to turn himself in to the cops and look at getting himself straightened out with the law, into rehab, and possibly out from under the threat of the man who was after him.

He agreed, but then started crying again.

"My daughter will spend Christmas without her dad. My dad was never there for me and I swore I would be a different daddy to my little girl." We sat in that library on that dark winter night with a man wrestling with all of his demons, holding him in the grace of God.

Finally, Gene spoke. "How about this? You go home tonight to your mother's house, spend Christmas with your daughter, and come back the day after Christmas and we'll call the cops together so we can tell them your story and advocate for some help for you?"

He agreed. Then, we asked him what he had to give his little girl for Christmas. A man stealing cameras from a church building in order to pay off a debt doesn't have spare spending money.

"Nothin'," he said.

"Well, we can't have that," Gene replied.

So, we went and found toys for his little girl among the toys we'd collected to give to needy families. We found a doll, a coloring set, hair accessories, and a game. While we were gathered in the library it had started to rain. Nickleby arrived at the church on his bike and the weather was no longer fit for riding, so Gene offered him a lift home. So they left together, Christmas turkey, presents for Nickleby's little girl, and all. We sent him home with those toys, food for Christmas dinner, and our prayers.

I was late getting home that night, my things-to-do list stretching out a mile long with Christmas and birthday tasks. But I had stood in the presence of God's grace that night, witnessed the sign that God's love is beyond understanding. In offering grace, I received grace, and I remembered once again what the miracle of Christmas really is.

Grace creeps in to the darkest corners of our lives and surprises us with its beauty, with its healing, with its love. The story of Christmas is a story of God saying to us, over and over again, "I love you."

Another song began playing in my mind. A song that we sang when I was a pastor at middle school summer camp. Middle schoolers, often so cool and resistant to showing their need for affection, requested this song over and over again. I can't remember any of the words except the chorus, sang as if God was speaking it, "I love you, I love you, I loooove you, I love you." The kids would sing that again and again, reminding themselves that no matter what, they are loved.

I felt as if God was singing that over us, in that church library on a dark and cold December night. "I love you, I love you, I loooove you." It was the song the angels sang to the shepherds, a message from God come down as the baby Jesus, "I love you, I love you, I looooove you, I love you." It was the song sung by the director of the play to that scared actor and it is the song that is sung whenever God's grace is given and received, when forgiveness is shared, when we remember the love that God has for each of us.

Nickleby came back the day after Christmas, ready to face the consequences of his actions. We decided not to press any charges, but he had other matters to talk over with the police. The deputy who came to take his report offered him the same grace we had and talked about how to help get his life back on track. We later learned that he made a plea deal for some of his other crimes. Rumor has it that he started rehab but didn't finish and has returned to petty theft.

Most of the time, when I think about that winter afternoon, I picture Nickleby like the shepherds in the Christmas story. Other times, however, I wonder if he wasn't the angel, come to proclaim God's good news to us in the church. We think we know the story, as we tell it every year, but seeing it lived is a whole different thing.

The day after Nickleby's visit to the church his mom called Gene and asked him why we had showed such kindness to her son.

Gene says he shrugged and said, "Its Christmas. Kids should see their dad on Christmas. Besides, we all make mistakes, and God hasn't finished with us yet."

She thanked him profusely and said that Nickleby had repeated over and over again after coming home, "I just don't know why they were so nice to me."

She told Gene that she didn't know if it would make any long-term difference in his life, but it had changed her life forever. "It was the best Christmas present you could have given me, having him here with his daughter. Thank you."

The funny thing, about good news, is that it travels. That is what the angels intended on that first Christmas so long ago. They told the good news to the shepherds and then sent them to find the baby and to keep sharing what they had experienced.

A few months later, I was on vacation in California. I pulled out of my in-laws' driveway. As I drove down their street, I could hear someone calling after me. I looked to see my husband's childhood friend and neighbor running after me. I stopped and rolled down the window.

"Thank you!" she said. Puzzled, I asked for what?

"I heard about the man at Christmas, at your church," she said. "I told all the people at work about it. You just don't hear enough stories like that. Thank you for caring about him even though he stole from you."

Grace interrupts our lives, reminds us what love feels like. It calls out the very best of who we are. It causes us to pause and hear the words, "I love you," spoken over our lives. The Christmas story interrupted history and proclaimed a love too wondrous to comprehend. When we witness that love, we are forever changed, left with the imprints on our soul. It causes us to tell others the story, like those shepherds so long ago who rushed to tell Mary what the angels had said about her little boy.

Star and angel will give the sign of the love that God has for us. That Advent, on that cold, wet afternoon, just a few days before Christmas an angel knocked at the church door with good news to share. God's love is here, now, and it is a gift for all of us.

Further Reflections

For I am convinced that neither death, nor life, nor angels, nor rulers, nor things present, nor things to come, nor powers, nor height, nor depth, nor anything else in all creation, will be able to separate us from the love of God in Christ Jesus our Lord.

Romans 8:38-39

When I share the story of Nickleby, one of the questions that I am frequently asked is this, "Why would a church have security cameras?" It is a great question that is tied in with grace, forgiveness, and healthy boundaries.

The church featured in the story runs a clothing bank that gives out over 30,000 pieces of clothing and household items per year. All of the items distributed through the clothing bank are donated by the community. In order to collect these items in an orderly manner, the church built a shed with a deposit chute. Imagine bank deposit chutes, only larger. Shortly after the shed was constructed, people began breaking into the shed. Sometimes they would come in through the chute, other times they would break the locks on the door. We quickly realized that it was expensive to replace door locks on a regular basis, and dangerous to have people squeezing through a chute designed for clothes, not humans.

We also became aware of other crimes happening on our property. In one instance, some men fleeing from the police stashed guns under the deck on the clothing bank building. Another time, while breaking into our clothing bank, a group of people were also shooting up on church property and left needles lying on the ground.

The clothing bank is committed to meeting the needs of the community through the distribution of free items, but we also recognized the need to set healthy boundaries and keep the larger neighborhood safe. So, we installed security cameras that allowed us to monitor activity and call the police when necessary.

This leads me to the next question. "If you forgive someone for theft, why call the police or monitor the property through security cameras in the first place?"

One of the biggest misconceptions about forgiveness is

that it means excusing or forgetting bad behavior. Forgiveness, in a spiritual sense of the word, is about releasing ill will and malice towards someone who has trespassed against you. It is not about releasing someone from the consequence of their actions. Forgiveness invites us to extend unearned and unmerited grace towards someone who has wronged us. Along the way, it sets us free from anger and bitterness.

Forgiveness is seeing someone as a whole human being, not just as the wrong that they committed. For example, instead of saying that someone is a liar, forgiveness helps us say, "Jane lied to me." Jane might also be a great mother, fantastic artist, and a good cook who lies. Her lying is not the entirety of who she is.

Forgiveness sets us free from thinking about revenge. For example, "I should call Jane up and tell her a giant lie so she can see how it feels!" Think about someone you might need to forgive. Most likely, you have had at least one or two thoughts about that person that are revenge thinking.

Now, there is a difference between revenge and consequences for actions. In the case of Jane, we might need to verify anything she tells us in the future.

In another example, if someone shares a confidence that we have entrusted to them, we might not share our secrets with them in the future. Those are normal consequences of broken trust. Revenge thinking would say we should go out and tell everyone all of the secrets we know about them.

Next, forgiveness asks that we move beyond revenge thinking to wishing the person well. We might say about Jane, I have a difficult time trusting her, but I hope that she has other friends that she is more honest with. Or, we might hope that Jane wins a cooking contest she has entered even though we are still hurt by the lie she told us.

Finally, we open ourselves up to be agents of good in the person's life. This doesn't mean we need to seek out someone who has hurt us. There might be times when we will never (or should never) see someone who has harmed us again. Think of crimes of violence or abuse. But, when given the opportunity to be an agent of good in the person's life, forgiveness invites us into that space.[6]

With Nickleby, the church advocated for him with the police. We were hoping that he might receive treatment for his addiction or other kinds of rehabilitation measures that could open opportunities in his future. It might look different in every situation, but the heart of this is listening for the whisper from God to be an advocate or person of good will in the life of the person who harmed you. This might be as simple as praying for them.

I no longer serve the church that showed such grace and forgiveness to Nickleby. I am working in a new church start in Olympia, Washington. Doing a new church start in the None Zone is daunting and at times seems almost foolish. Often, that is the case with following a call from God.

When I find myself discouraged, and wondering what the church has to offer to a world that so often rejects it, I remember Nickleby. I think of what it means when someone encounters grace for the first time and how life is never the same after. I think of forgiveness, and how difficult, life-giving, and necessary it is. Grace and forgiveness are certainly found outside the doors of church. But the church also has a great gift to offer the world in being a place whose primary business is grace, forgiveness, and love, and risk-taking advocacy for others.

---

6   Smedes, Lewis B., The Art of Forgiving. New York City: Ballantine Boos, 1997

In the None Zone it can be easy to fall into a scarcity mentality. We can look around and see brunch spots filled to the brim on a Sunday morning while our pews sit empty. We can lament how much we need people to come into our doors.

But that is to mistake the purpose of the gospel. The church doesn't need the world as much as the world needs the church in its most authentic, beautiful self as a grace giving, mercy extending, loving group of called people who want to bless others because we have been blessed. The gospel is abundant and the grace we have to share is meant to pour out from our doors into a world that is longing to receive it.

Rev. Heather Sparkman did not grow up Christian. She walked into a United Methodist Church in Washington State at age twenty-eight and felt like she had come home! She has been in church every Sunday since then and answered the call to become a pastor nine years ago. She attended Claremont School of Theology where she received a diverse and challenging education and earned her Master of Divinity degree. Currently, she is planting a church in Olympia, Washington, the heart of the None Zone and she loves seeing God at work in the most unexpected places. Heather lives with her amazing husband, who is not Christian, three fantastic kids, and too many pets to list!

Discussion Questions

Chapter 4: Grace Interrupted
By Rev. Heather Sparkman

What is so remarkable about forgiveness?

When have you given or received forgiveness?

How do you understand "God's grace?"

CHAPTER FIVE

All Are Welcome!

By Rev. Kelly Dahlman-Oeth

"… I was a stranger and you welcomed me …"

– Matthew 25:35 (NRSV)

Under the darkness of dawn, I arrived at church on Sunday morning as I often do. Still, I could make out the distinct piles of desperate souls wrapped in blankets and sleeping bags on the deck at the back entrance to the church. I tensed up at the thought of having to pick up bits of orange peel and trash I saw on the sidewalk. I announced myself as I headed up the steps, "G'MORNING GUYS!"

I hadn't slept well, and my mood was sour. I realized too late that I sounded like I was waking up teenagers who were going to miss school because they overslept. "IT'S TIME TO GET UP! I NEED YOU TO START PICKING UP!"

Sophia and Juan sat up and started gathering their belongings that had spilled out of their backpacks through the night. I unlocked the back doors and invited them to come in to get warm and use the bathroom. Softening a bit, I said, "I'll get some coffee going after I put my bag down."

I unlocked the back doors and headed toward the front door leading out to the front courtyard. The noise and wind from Aurora Avenue's four lanes make the front of the building less desirable, but not enough this morning. Huddled under the narrow overhang, as close to the sanctuary doors as possible, I saw the single blue sleeping bag flanked by two large black duffle bags. A worn-out, ten-speed bicycle that still had enough paint to see that it used to be white kept watch over it all.

I didn't recognize the bike, the bags, or the blue sleeping bag. "Hey buddy, I have to have you get up now, but you can come inside and get warm." From the top of the sleeping bag emerged an unshaven, sleepy-eyed face with a hint of a smile that offered the gentlest, "Good morning. How are you?" It was the first of many mornings that Eric would greet me that way.

As we talked over coffee, I invited them all to stay for worship, certain that their presence was at the same time the presence of Christ.

Over the next few weeks, I'd learn Eric's story. After living the last seventeen years in the same apartment building in Everett, the building was sold, and the new owners gave the tenants a "notice to vacate" for remodeling. Following the brief remodel, the rent was increased 50 percent. Eric, along with most of the other tenants, could not afford to return.

Eric is fifty-five years old and disabled. Along with his "notice to vacate," these two factors resulted in what amounts to a golden ticket in the homeless community. He has a transferable Section 8 voucher, a housing subsidy paid by the federal government directly to the landlord. In theory, finding housing for him should be even easier since he has never struggled with addiction or alcoholism.

I spent the next twelve weeks learning more than I ever wanted to know about the unnecessarily slow, bureaucratic processes of two different housing authority systems. During that same time, Eric would end up in the emergency room three times to be treated and immediately released for pneumonia and other respiratory complications resulting from his chronic obstructive pulmonary disease (COPD).

I'm incredibly blessed to serve the community of Shoreline, Washington with the beloved community at Ronald United Methodist Church. In the two years that I've been serving our community with them, most of them have come to understand that when I say "congregation," I may be referring to the faithful who gather on Sunday morning for worship, or I may be talking about my friends that I invite in for coffee. I experienced a little cognitive dissonance when I arrived. The congregation had just been through a lengthy discernment process that resulted in selling part of the property and creating a unique partnership with two non-profits, Compass Housing Alliance and Hopelink.

That vision of that partnership is now a physical reality. Compass Housing Alliance's Ronald Commons has sixty units of permanent housing for low and very low income, including formerly homeless, individuals and families.

Hopelink of Shoreline was able to move from a 5000 square-foot space they were leasing into a 12,500 square-foot space that now houses a food bank built like a grocery store, and offices and classrooms where they support the community with employment specialists, emergency assistance, ESL classes, life skills coaching, and more.

The congregation at Ronald United Methodist Church supported that vision and made it possible literally in their "back yard." That's why I was surprised when I first arrived and learned that they had a practice of keeping the exterior doors locked except during worship.

Despite their vision and desire to provide housing and services to the most vulnerable, some had fears about persons

who were struggling with homelessness, addiction, and/
or mental illness. As is often the case, it was a fear of the
unknown. Having been steeped in years of Bible Study, their
hearts and minds had been open to God's call. But the doors
remained locked because most of them had limited experience,
and few or no relationships, with these "other" children of
God.

In my experience, hearts and minds are much harder to
unlock, and require the work of the Ultimate Locksmith. Once
hearts and minds are unlocked, doors are easy.

Within months, the open hearts, minds, and doors led
most of the faithful members to see that there is little value
distinguishing between those in the congregation who live in
houses and those who don't. Whether it's Eric or some other
stranger who wanders in off the street, the gentle souls who
gather weekly for Bible Study are quick to welcome them to sit
down and stay for lunch.

Some of our friends come in and participate in the discussion, others have been known to doze off until lunch. Whether
exhausted from a sleepless night or numbed from a chemical
they've managed to buy to block out the pain of their life, I'm
grateful these weary souls have found a place and a people
who will watch over them while they rest. Those who don't
want to stay are still given the lunch that's been brought to
share.

It's the same when the United Methodist Women's *Martha's
Circle* gather each month. I've walked by their meeting more
than once to see Eric sitting at the table like an honored guest.
While he may attend regularly, Eric obviously won't become
a member of the United Methodist Women's group, but he and
others are active participants in the life of the congregation,
and we are quickly becoming part of their lives.

This week, Eric will sign a lease for an apartment less than a mile from the church. He is excited to be so close to the church but concerned that he may start to isolate himself. I assured him that his church family is already starting to gather furnishings and is eager to come for a house warming.

We've learned that these encounters are never one-way transactions. We are not givers or receivers. No, each of us come with something to offer and each us come with some need. Like Paul's description of the body of Christ, some of us may seem more vulnerable. While God calls us to give more honor to these members of the body, we are all to have the same care for one another, for we are all equal before God.

On any given Sunday the body of Christ that gathers will be made up of the housed and unhoused, retired and just tired. Someone's BMW will be parked not far from someone's grocery cart. Addicts, recovering addicts, and those of us who still try to hide our more socially acceptable addictions will sing from the same hymnal.

Black, brown, and white folks will spend several minutes greeting one another while the praise team sings. When I stand up for the sermon, I will do my best to greet them in as many native tongues as they represent, because this body of Christ that gathers to worship just north of Seattle didn't just grow up in Shoreline. Most Sundays, I look at these blessed saints and I think of the Holy Spirit blowing over the pilgrims at Pentecost. The global community is Filipino, Kenyan, Zimbabwean, Lithuanian, Ghanaian, Tongan, and more.

Filipino Lolas and Lolos will take turns holding babies. Young adults will play peek-a-boo with the preschoolers peeking over the pews. My Ates (aunties) keep the church pantry stocked with coffee, cream, and sugar for our morning guests who spent the night outside.

I don't worry that Eric will become isolated, because he is part of the body of Christ in this place. He is part of us, and while some of us may only think that Eric needs us, according to Jesus, we are the ones who need Eric. Our understanding of Christianity, nay our experience of Christ, is bound up in our willingness to welcome the stranger.

I've been around enough churches announcing "All are welcome" on the sign out front, the banner on their web page, and the cover of the bulletin. Without announcing it anywhere, these beautiful souls at Ronald United Methodist Church have shown me what welcome looks like day after day.

Postscript

If you worried that Eric might cloister himself in his new apartment, fear not. Two months later, he still comes to the church several times each week to worship with us, visit with his Bible study friends, and help clean up the place he temporarily called home.

We continue to learn with Eric and others, that God's beloved community was never intended to look homogenous, and the spaces we inhabit were never intended to be reserved and preserved for Sunday morning activities. Having learned that we can find ways to embrace and support our unhoused siblings, we have opened our building to shelter ten of God's beloved children.

As they struggle with the often overwhelming obstacles of chronic and recurring trauma, homelessness, addiction, poverty, and more, we are learning how to form a beloved community with them. Through our fledgling efforts, we continue to build trust with one another allowing for relationships grounded in love.

Nightly, the housed and unhoused sit together for a

"family meal," sharing the best and worst of the day. Hosts come to spend the night to make a place for our siblings to be safe, dry, and warm. Those with washing machines at home pick up a few extra loads each week to launder, fold, and return to those "housed" in the church. A "court clothes closet" began out of a need for our friends who are trying to clean up their record of misdemeanor charges that are often heaped up on those who are poor. Together, we go to court to stand before the prosecutor and judge as a sign of support and loving solidarity.

In the fertile soil of these loving relationships, the Holy Spirit continues to transform lives. Some have sought recovery programs to work toward sobriety. One young man has found a new community of friends who love him and support him in his sobriety. He has moved into housing and is eager to begin to put his life back together.

We who are housed continue to learn how much we need our brothers and sisters. Through them we see the depth of our spiritual need. Together, we yearn to grow in love in the house of Christ's love that has a welcome mat as wide as heaven.

Reverend Kelly Dahlman-Oeth serves the community of Shoreline, Washington as the lead pastor at Ronald United Methodist Church. After receiving his Master of Divinity Degree from Candler School of Theology at Emory University, he served for six years in higher education administration in two United Methodist Seminaries: Candler School of Theology and Garrett-Evangelical Theological Seminary.

He returned to local church ministry in 1999 and served for eight years at Browns Point United Methodist Church in Tacoma Washington. In 2007, he was appointed to serve the community of Kirkland at Lake Washington United Methodist Church. While there, he and leaders of the Lake Washington United Methodist Church assisted a group of forty "unhoused" individuals in setting up a semi self-sustaining encampment community. The leadership then established a unique Safe Parking program for women and families living in vehicles.

The church partnered with participants to provide access to the kitchen, bathrooms, community rooms, phones, storage, etc. By building relationships and community, over 150 households moved from their vehicles into transitional or permanent shelter in four years. As an advocate and agent for change, he strives to build relationships and community between his siblings who are housed and those who live without adequate shelter.

Discussion Questions

Chapter 5: All Are Welcome
By Rev. Kelly Dahlman-Oeth

What did the author mean when he said, "We are the ones who need Eric?"

Sunday mornings have been called "the most segregated time of the week," but this congregation appears to be very diverse. What are the challenges and the blessings of being amongst a diverse population?

CHAPTER SIX

The Second Half
of the Movie

By Rev. Meredith Dodd

*[18] There is no fear in love, but perfect love casts out fear; for fear
has to do with punishment, and whoever fears has not reached
perfection in love. [19] We love because he first loved us.*

– 1 John 4:18-19 (NSRV)

From a very young age, my son has been obsessed
with *The Sound of Music*. At first, he fell in love with the
soundtrack. We sang "Edelweiss" as a lullaby, and he memorized all of Maria's favorite things, not just the raindrops on
roses and whiskers on kittens. When he got a little older, he
was thrilled to discover that *The Sound of Music* was also a
movie, and he was delighted to discover that Maria sang "My
Favorite Things" so she could reassure the children during a
thunderstorm.

For a long time, I would stop the video after the first half
of the movie, before Maria and her family are chased by the
Nazis and have to flee the country as refugees. But when my
son grew a little older, I decided it was time to show him the
whole story, even the scary parts. And he was shocked at the
idea that soldiers could be so bad that they might even want to
hurt children.

I thought I had pushed him too far. But after we watched
the movie a few more times, my son stopped being surprised,
even by the traitor who tells the Nazis where the family is. I

decided it was time that we talked about the role of the nuns and the church. "The church is where the children go to hide," I told him, "and when the family needs protection, the church stands up to the bad soldiers." It was hard to expose him to something so fearful. But when I told him, "The church helps people not be afraid of the bad guys," I was the one who started to cry.

Here in the Pacific Northwest, the Nazis haven't taken over (although just like every part of the U.S., we've got our fair share of them). But in many ways, we are so filled with fear that it is as if we live under a totalitarian regime. Sometimes, we try to shield ourselves from that fear by skipping the scary parts of our lives, by letting people see only the parts where we feel like we have everything under control. Other times, the fear overcomes us like a tidal wave, and we drown in our sense of hopelessness, the feeling that our lives are meaningless because nothing we say or do seems to make any difference to the world around us. Here in the Pacific Northwest, fear pretty much defines our culture. How, then, shall we live?

Scripture tells us that "perfect love casts out all fear." The United Methodist tradition tells us that God calls us to love more and more perfectly until we can love as God loves us. And much like that abbey near the mountains in Austria, the church calls us to stand up to the fear by gathering people into community, proclaiming radical hope in the midst of a hopeless, fear-filled culture.

Sometimes, churches remember this calling only when they face a public challenge to continuing business as usual. One of our church's most active members lived in a homeless encampment. As a leader in the encampment and in our congregation, he came to us with a proposal: the encampment needed a new place to stay for three months, and he would like our congregation to host them in the church's parking lot.

The church hemmed and hawed. We had many fears. *What if our neighbors got angry at us? What if people stopped coming to church?* The deadline drew near. Finally, we decided to be brave: we would hold a congregational vote on whether or not to host the encampment. After much discussion and prayer, we decided unanimously to host. We ended the meeting singing the hymn, "Here I Am, Lord," which proclaims, "I will go, Lord, if you lead me. I will hold your people in my heart."

Our fears came true. The neighbors were not thrilled. At times, some were so angry that we thought their threats would erupt into violence. For some in the congregation, the tents in the parking lot were an inconvenience, an eyesore, and sometimes even a source of fear. But we persisted in love, listening deeply, praying for those who considered themselves our enemies, and working alongside our homeless brothers and sisters to find solutions on how to live together.

We brought food, supplies, and materials for setting up the tents. Charity was easy. But sharing space with someone meant loving them intimately, not just offering basic kindness from a distance. This kind of love proved more difficult. On a cold night, someone was invited to sleep inside, only to vomit all over the newly-cleaned carpet. One person talked so much that the church staff had trouble getting work done. Some in the community were less than eager to chip in to help, and tension arose between those who did most of the manual labor and those who chose to sit instead. We learned that if we wanted to love, we had to embrace conflict, remembering that sometimes Jesus got annoyed and even angry with the people God gave him to love.

As the encampment stayed longer, we turned to the

community for support. We were surprised and delighted
to find that God gave us more opportunities to choose love
instead of fear. We developed an ongoing relationship with
a group of Muslims who came to support the encampment,
hosting a dinner to learn more about their work to alleviate
extreme poverty. We received donations from a Jewish neighbor, who wrote to say that this was the first time in seventy
years she had ever given money to a Christian organization.

Eventually the encampment moved on. We were
exhausted, a little grumpy and grateful for the respite from
what we learned is a very challenging area of ministry. But
the relationships we built, both with the homeless and the
housed, changed our hearts, filling them with a love which
crowded out our fear. And we had begun to learn that this
kind of transforming love was already at work beyond our
church walls, and that we could join more fully in God's work
when we set down our need to always be the ones in charge.

I don't think most of us ever understood what it meant to
live outside in a tent. But to a certain extent, being in daily
contact with people on the margins reminded our church what
it means for a human being to be vulnerable. Vulnerability
can be scary, not only because you might get hurt, but because
you might be judged for not having your act together, you
might discover the hopelessness of being the only one suffering the way that you are.

Choosing vulnerability is difficult; we want to maintain
our facades. But for many of us, this choice softens our hearts
just enough so that once again, God's love can begin to crowd
out our fear. In my ministry, I encounter many people whose
lives are pretty much safe. Because they want to maintain the
illusion of safety, they are terrified to rely on other people for
help, let alone to rely on God's grace. When they do encoun-

ter something unexpected – the loss of a job, the end of a marriage, a life-limiting diagnosis – they are tempted to hide how overwhelmed they are, to pretend that they can do it all by themselves. And when they choose to shatter this illusion, love comes flooding in.

In our church, the most overwhelmed people were the caregivers. Some cared for adult children with profound disabilities, others cared for their spouses with dementia, others were dealing with the unpredictability of Parkinson's. After listening to enough stories of desperation, we started a caregivers' group. Mostly, we talked, but the group kept itself grounded in Christian spirituality by praying for one another's families, by praying through the psalms of lament, and by commending one another for the small everyday acts of love, even when they seemed utterly pointless.

The group began mired in hopelessness, in the fear that nothing they did mattered when they cared for loved ones who could not express appreciation in return. By the end of our allotted time, however, the group had not only enfolded people new to the community, they insisted that they should continue to meet because they could mirror the belief that love is as strong as death, even when they could neither see nor believe it themselves.

The caregivers' vulnerability broke open the fearful hearts of the congregation as well. In order to support the caregivers' group, the congregation decided they would offer a separate "class" for the care receivers, people with serious medical disabilities. The class was often simple, involving puzzles or a CD of familiar songs or playing volleyball with a balloon. Eventually, there were more teachers for this class than there were students. The caregivers reported that they had not seen their care receivers that lively all week. Even the youth, many of whom had never been around a person living with dementia, sought out connection in a way they had not done before.

This willingness to move past the fear of vulnerability began in these classes, but the spiritual practices we tried out there soon spread to the larger congregation. The old Methodist question, "How is it with your soul?" opened many of our meetings. At first, people answered simply, "It is well," or often, "My soul is very tired," but eventually the congregation developed a practice of shared vulnerability, answering about what troubled them, what small victories gave them hope, even what disciplines they were struggling to cultivate in their everyday lives. During Sunday worship, immediately following the sermon, I would ask the congregation an open-ended question that invited them to connect the sermon to their experience of God in the world. At first the questions were simple, things like, "What do you thank God for right now?"

But over time, they grew in spiritual complexity, until it wasn't unusual to hear a question like, "In today's Scripture, Jesus asks someone if they truly want to be made well. When you search your heart, in what ways do you want to be healed? In what ways do you want the world around you to be healed?" After several months, the congregation began to respond after the sermon with their own spontaneous testimonies about where they sensed the movement of the Holy Spirit. On some Sundays, once they started talking, it was hard to get them to stop!

Cultivating the kind of love that can cast out fear requires a lot of work and even more humility. To love our communities, we must know our communities, listening deeply to the people we like, the people who scare us, and the people who consider us the enemy. To love in this way, we also have to release our insistence on success. Perfect love casts out fear, but it neither takes away the challenging circumstances we face nor promises good-looking statistics on church growth. When we reclaim the hope of resurrection, we are able to set aside our fear of death, a practice which embodies the gospel for the people around us, a different way of living in a world which exalts growth and buries weakness in shame. When the world tries to get us to seek a more perfect appearance or a more perfect performance, we turn instead toward becoming more perfect in the way we love. When we are unafraid to be vulnerable, our hearts become soft enough to love the fearful, the imperfect, and the vulnerable, and we discover that it is exactly these things that draw us together as human beings.

The next time you watch *The Sound of Music*, I encourage you not to skip the scary parts. Singing about your favorite things can give you a little comfort. But if you watch the second half of the movie, the part where things start to get really scary, you will also catch a glimpse of the love that gives us courage to protect the vulnerable, to come out of hiding, and never to be afraid of the bad guys.

Rev. Meredith Dodd serves as pastor of Bryn Mawr United Methodist Church, a small multicultural parish in Seattle, WA. She holds an M.Div. from Seattle University, an M.A. in Education from Stanford, and a B.A. in English from Yale. Before becoming a pastor, Meredith taught high school and college English, working primarily with immigrant and refugee students. She and her son recently attended a Sound of Music singalong dressed as Maria and Captain Von Trapp.

Discussion Questions

Chapter 6:
The Second Half of the Movie
Rev. Meredith Dodd

Where do you see fear and desperation in your community?

Where do people facing those fears and desperations go for support?

In what ways do you want the world around you to be healed?

CHAPTER SEVEN

Acceptance and Transformation

By Rev. Bradley Beeman

*And let us consider how to provoke one
another to love and good deeds...*

– Hebrews 10:24 (NSRV)

Her name is translated as Mary. She is eleven years old. Because of malnutrition suffered throughout her life she has been unable to place either one of her heels on the ground. Her muscles, ligaments, and tendons were unable to develop properly, so she walks on her toes unable to lower her feet to the ground. She has no parents. They were killed in a raid; one of the multiple raids in her village in Myanmar. She escaped with two older siblings as the shooting began. They found their way through the jungle, swam the river that borders Myanmar and Thailand, and were found on the shore by villagers on the Thailand side. The children were hungry, thirsty, malnourished, and terrified. They had nothing. By this time, Mary could hardly walk. She is now connected to the greater Seattle area in ways that she can hardly believe, particularly to a church.

Her name is Marin. She was born without the artery that connects her left lung to her heart. As you can imagine, it has caused severe challenges for her and for her parents. Her mother is a nurse. Her father is a consultant for the Navy. They live and work in Seattle and weren't sure where to turn once this precious child was born, and more specifically where they could turn for love and support. They prayed and then found a place here in the greater Seattle area.

His name was Song Lee. He was four years old at the time. He and his family had just moved to the Seattle area from Korea. Song Lee's father works in the tech industry and his job brought him to the greater Seattle area. His parents knew that the educational standards here were among the highest in the country. Song Lee's mom stayed home to care for the three children. The children spoke no English when they arrived. The parents began to search for a place where, without judgment, their youngest might learn, not only the language, but the culture, of their new home. They hoped to find a place that would affirm and support their hopes, beliefs, and expectations. They are Christian, and they found that place.

There is Naomi, a single mom living in her car with an eighteen-month-old child. There is Matt, a young man who had just moved to the area from California and was entering middle school. He was shy, small, and anxious about entering a place where he knew no one. There is Jim, a recently retired aerospace engineer who helped design the International Space Station. He was looking for a place where he could simply be himself and share with others about his life. There is Marie, the head of a fast-growing start-up company looking for connections and a place where she can deepen her faith. They all have things in common.

First, all but little Mary live here, in the None Zone, the greater Seattle area in the western portion of the State of Washington. The None Zone is known as a place that lacks religious focus. We're better known for our Birkenstocks, our rain, and our coffee, rather than our faith. Churches are thought to be dying and the assumption is that nobody wants anything to do with "church." It's true that many around us see the local church or organized religion as dogmatic, judgmental, and irrelevant. There are many who live here who pride themselves on not attending church and self-identify as "spiritual but not religious." The outdoors is thought to be a sanctuary, and the weekends are a time to escape from the extreme pressures of working at Microsoft, Boeing, Amazon, or Google. Yet, there is more here than meets the eye.

There are actions that center around faith and practice, actions that represent Jesus, and opportunities to deepen our own faith. Faith, action, practice, and Jesus are but a few of the things that tie those names together. Maybe more unexpectedly, the other thing that ties every one of the above-mentioned stories together is, in fact, a church. It is a church called Aldersgate, a church located in the southern portion of Bellevue, a large city just east of Seattle, a church that sits in the middle of the None Zone. Within a ten-mile radius of Aldersgate are the corporate offices of T-Mobile, Amazon, Google, Microsoft, Boeing, and multiple start-ups. Bellevue is a dynamic place, and unlike some of the other areas around us, this part of the greater Seattle area is wealthy. Bill Gates lives nearby.

The average home has just crossed the million-dollar mark, and people speaking Mandarin Chinese alongside two dialects of East Indian have become the fastest growing populations, all tied to the emerging and growing tech industry. Ninety (plus) first languages are spoken in that ten-mile radius, and all the complexities that surround so many emerging cultures are present. So why would anyone need a church? More importantly, why would anyone attend or become a part of a church? Let me share some additions to the stories mentioned above.

Mary was taken in by a family from the village of Mae Sot, Thailand. The father of the family was friends with Kara, a woman working with a village just north of Mae Sot. She was working with a non-governmental organization assisting that village in increasing their understanding of sustainable farming. Kara grew up at Aldersgate. Her parents and even her grandparents attend. Kara heard Mary's story, had a vision, and she contacted me. She knew the individual stories of hundreds of children who had fled the violence in Myanmar. She knew the passion of this church around mission was to help transform the lives of those in need. She sent me a picture of her dream; a really rough drawing of a boarding house. It was to be a boarding house for orphaned children, and she wondered if Aldersgate could take on such a project 10,000 miles from here.

I offered the opportunity to the church. They jumped at the chance and committed to providing whatever was needed to build and supply Kara's dream. A year later I was able to fly to Mae Sot and offer a blessing for the now built and functioning boarding house. It was named Grace, Grace Boarding House. It was designed by Kara's father, Wally, an engineer, and built by four men. Three were from the local village of Mae Sot, and one was my oldest son. He and Wally had traveled to help in the construction. The result: thirty children found a safe place to call home. Other boarding houses have now been built in the area, all of which offer safety and a home for orphaned children. The love, the finances, the support, the prayer, even some of the labor was provided by this church. Lives have been saved, including little Mary's.

I will never forget inviting her to come and sit with me as I shared a story with her. On tiptoes she came up, crawled into my lap, and changed my life, and she has changed the lives of everyone else in this small church with a big heart, this church called Aldersgate.

Now closer to home. Marin's dad comes from a very religious family in the South. Marin's mom became pregnant before they were married. They knew the pregnancy was a challenge but wouldn't know specifics until the birth. Part of their family believed God to be so judgmental that He would cause this abnormality. Marin's parents were terrified and wondered if all of this was some kind of curse from God. Their friends shared that it was why they didn't go to church. This family found Aldersgate. I did their wedding; a very small affair in South Seattle when mom was a month from giving birth. We were at the hospital the day Marin was born. The church surrounded this young family with love and prayer. I will never forget the day little Marin was baptized in the Aldersgate sanctuary.

There was no hiding her physical challenges. That said, this loving community of faith took this small family into their embrace and shared a love the family didn't expect to find in any church, especially a church in the Seattle area. Marin continues to struggle as do her mom and dad. But they have found a family that will not let them go. It's the kind of faith, the kind of love we believe to be present in this community, in this area, and in those who seek to follow Jesus right here in Seattle.

But there is more.

Song Lee is one of 155 children that attend the Aldersgate Christian Preschool. His family was drawn to it by the name, and stayed because of the love, acceptance, and faith of its director and staff. I remember the day Song Lee voluntarily approached his teacher, his mother in tow. It was the first time he'd ever done anything like this. I was there doing my normal walk-through of the classrooms. Song Lee let go of the hand of his mother, faced the teacher, crossed his arms over his chest, bowed deeply, and then in perfect English said, "My name in English is Sebastian." His teacher clapped and then hugged him. His mom wept. I smiled and offered a prayer of thanksgiving with his mom. The transformation continues as our preschool continues to love and accept all who come through our doors. We seek to help families keep their cultures of origin yet learn about the cultures of this part of the country. For us, it's based first in our love of Christ and second in what we believe Christ taught us about community, encouragement, and acceptance. Suffice it to say that the Aldersgate Christian Preschool is full to capacity with waiting lists in most classes. That's not too bad for the None Zone.

Regarding the others mentioned above, they found us because of a website, but stayed because of the love this place continuously seeks to share. Naomi and her son know they have a place where they can come and be safe. They can find food, financial support, and other kinds of support for both of them. Matt found a youth group that continues to grow; a group that offered him a place of acceptance, encouragement, and grace. Jim found himself surrounded by other aeronautical engineers: folks who speak the same language, share the same interests, and share a similar history.

Inasmuch as I can't understand a word they say, it's been fun to watch them gather at coffee hour after worship and swap stories. More importantly, it's been a privilege to watch them step up and rebuild the roof of a parishioner in need, do repairs at church, and mentor some of the younger engineers now living in our area.

And finally there is Marie. She has found a place of networking, and not just the kind of networking that allows a businessperson to increase their bottom line. Marie has found other creative minds who support her, and even help her ask the right questions. More importantly, she has found a group of other businesswomen who pray with her as each seeks to be Christ in the ever-challenging world of business in this area.

Aldersgate is not a big church, particularly by the standards of other places across the country and around the world. Yet Aldersgate has a heart for mission and outreach. This church is transforming lives: the lives of orphans, immigrants, families facing illness, families facing homelessness, individuals of all ages and stages of life looking for a place to belong. Again, all of this in the None Zone.

We certainly wear our Birkenstocks, and certainly drink our coffee. We certainly believe we live in the most beautiful place in the world, partially because of, and partially in spite of, the rain. More importantly we are a place that seeks to love in the name of Jesus, to offer actions of God's love to everyone and anyone in need. We seek to live up to our name. Aldersgate was the place where our founder, John Wesley's heart was "strangely warmed" by the Spirit of God. We seek to do the same, sharing the love of God in the None Zone and throughout God's creation.

Bradley Beeman is the child of two courageous parents who, throughout their lives, took stands around issues of justice, freedom, and social action. He and his siblings, each in their own way, have sought to define their lives with similar actions.

Brad learned to build hand-hewn log homes without power tools. While using this knowledge to establish three businesses, he served as a youth director at churches in Washington and California. A passion for protecting children and youth and preventing drug abuse led to a position as National Director of Community Support for Developmental Research and Programs, a research and development firm that worked alongside the Social Development Research Group at the University of Washington. Brad traveled the country talking about risk and protective factors related to children and youth. He spoke to then Gov. Bill Clinton, Sen. Al Gore, served on two D.C. task forces around international drug abuse and drug violence, and parenting as prevention.

It was while holding a cocaine-addicted baby at Howard University Hospital in Washington DC, that Brad felt an overwhelming call to ministry. He has been in ministry for the past twenty-six years, serving in urban, suburban, and rural Washington, and in urban (Los Angeles and Santa Monica) Southern California. Brad seeks to bring each piece of his life experiences to his ministry, his community, his colleagues, and his family.

Discussion Questions

Chapter 7:
Acceptance and Transformation
By Rev. Bradley Beeman

Aldersgate Christian Preschool welcomes children from all faith backgrounds, or no faith background at all. What compelled them to do this?

Where do you see diversity in your community?

How does diversity help a church grow their faith?

CHAPTER EIGHT
God Saw and It Was Good
By Rev. Jan Bolerjack

God looked over everything that had been made;
it was so good, so very good!

– Genesis 1:31 (author's interpretation)

These words are part of the foundation of our faith. These words are spoken to each of God's creations – the sun and the moon, the land and the sea, the birds and the beasts, the humans – YES the humans. It is ALL good.

"You are a beloved Child of God. You are created in the image of God. And God said, 'It is good, so very good.'"

I use this language often when meeting homeless individuals that arrive at my church campus looking for assistance. Usually they are asking for money or other tangible resources and I can at times assist them with those, but I am mostly taken by their response to the language of worth and attitude of kindness. That is what their faces often show to be the biggest surprise and as such, the greatest need.

Many of the folks I work with feel like they have let others down, been tossed aside by society, have some intrinsic shortcoming that makes them less of a human, and/or made grave mistakes. They feel they can never recover to a stable life. Their self-worth has been shattered. They live in the shadows, in crime-ridden hotels, in nearby woods, in risky and dangerous relationships, or on someone else's couch. They sometimes make choices for survival that put them at risk of danger for health or freedom.

Mental illness is rampant in the people I meet. Unable to manage the health care systems, appointments, medications – they wander the streets trying to cope and stay out of trouble. They report that most other people don't look them in the eye or even speak to them. Food is found in dumpsters behind restaurants or through a series of community meals where nobody knows your name. The opportunity for a shower is pure ecstasy.

"You are a beloved Child of God. You are created in the image of God. And God said, 'It is good, so very good.'"

These words spoken aloud to a person with no self-worth or societal recognition can fall on unhearing ears. They can be discarded as easily as the hurtful words that are often thrown at them. These words don't make sense in the world in which they live.

My experience, though, is that if these words are shared often enough and with enough sincerity they can start to imprint and make a difference. At first, "Yeah right." Then, "What difference does it make?" Later, "Could it be true?" Finally, "YES!" And then their whole countenance changes. They stand taller, they speak with more confidence, they show up more often, they start to give back. Life's situation may not change but attitude can affect change dramatically.

I find people come back for more and more affirmation of their place with God. They need to believe and can only do so by hearing it more and more. The world has worn them down but faith can bring them back up. Our God language can make the difference. Our attitudes change their attitudes about themselves and their place in the world.

On the campus of Riverton Park United Methodist Church

in Tukwila, Washington we meet many people who have complex barriers to a full life. Our community is known to include many families and individuals that are very low income, recent immigrants just adjusting to life in the United States, those who are drug and alcohol addicted, and those living in generational poverty. This has proven to be a rich environment for ministry using Genesis 1:31.

Through our Food Pantry, Homeless Ministry, Tukwila Kids Make Music, Community meals, and Sunday worship we are able to connect with a lot of people. Our mission springs from the needs of the community around us. We have embraced the practice of being the heart, hands, and voice of Christ using words of welcome and acceptance and a sharing of resources. It is a congregation-wide practice.

We work closely with city leaders, including the mayor and city council, police, and the school district to identify needs and develop responses. The local police often bring us families living without shelter or those in unsafe situations. The school social workers refer families facing homelessness. The congregation welcomes and works with them to engage other social services to move them on with stability.

We have secured grants to fund a case manager to work specifically with homeless families and a musician to offer music lessons to kids whose families would not be able to afford them. We know that music is often a key to greater success in school.

Over the years we have found ways to not turn any at-risk families away. At times many rooms in the church have been filled with homeless children and their adults. We also have large tents with heat, houses, car camping, and motor homes for temporary housing. All people are accorded dignity and worth and given a chance for stability.

There was a time when our local police officers were faced with enforcing an eviction notice for a mom with two children. She had been working steadily and paying rent according to her lease for three years when her younger child was diagnosed with cancer. Over the next few months as she tried to get her daughter to her medical appointments she lost more and more time at work, had less income and got behind in both utilities and rent. The apartment manager had no other choice than to evict her and her kids. The officers brought her and the kids to us.

She was frightened. She was defeated. She was feeling very hopeless. She thought she was going to lose her kids and kept asking, "Why? What have I done to deserve this?" She felt as if she had done something wrong and her family was suffering. She felt as if it was punishment and that there was not hope for her. She had worn out her family and friends with her needs. She was all alone.

This was a family falling on hard times, with very little recourse. Fortunately, we were able to give her respite, which allowed her to gather her strength and confidence again. We believed in her. We met with her every week – at first suggesting baby steps until she was able to step out on her own again. We helped her get the resources she needed to make sure the kids were adequately cared for. That in itself boosted her self-esteem. After a couple of months of staying with us, she was able to pull the resources together to get a new apartment. She left us standing tall and confident.

At one point a middle-aged man well known to the community as mentally ill started hanging around. At first, he would sit in our social hall and charge his phone all day. Then he set up a tent and stayed on the property with our other campers. All the while, talking loudly to himself and reporting thoughts that to us seemed less than plausible. He self-admitted to being schizophrenic but didn't like taking his meds so he was med free. Some days he would just wander around talking out loud. Other days he would engage with whoever would listen to his sagas about people stealing from his bank account or his family's denial of his existence. We wanted to help him but mostly we just wanted to treat him like a human being of worth and dignity. We signed him up for mental and physical health care, but he was not able to follow through or keep the appointments made. It was not that he was defiant. He just couldn't do it.

Some days when he would be a distraction to the other work going on here, he would be asked to leave. But he always came back looking for the affirmation and warmth he received here. He was even able to tell us that. He reported over and over to us that nowhere else that he went was he really welcomed. Nowhere else did people know his name. Nowhere else did people smile when they saw him. It breaks my heart how many times I have heard that over the years.

The members of this church have been highly energized in this ministry. They have been quick to learn what a difference it makes to treat all people with dignity and to use our resources to assist those who are struggling. They have been able to overlook some of the consequences of working with people with mental illness and those who are just down and out. Missing dishware and dirty bathrooms are not as important as welcome and acceptance. Material possessions can be replaced, human beings cannot.

The church may not be able to solve all the issues involved with inequalities in our society but we can change the way people feel about themselves and those around them. It starts with our very creation. God saw it, and it was good.

Reverend Jan Bolerjack is a United Methodist Elder who has served urban and suburban churches in the Pacific Northwest since 1992. She is currently in her 11th year at Riverton Park UMC in Tukwila, WA, a high poverty, transient, diverse population near SeaTac airport.

Ministry at RPUMC involves a vital worshipping/learning community: a food pantry that feeds 400 households each week, a community dinner program, shelter for the homeless in tents, houses, and in the church building, a community garden for recently-settled immigrants, free music programs for children, and case management for those facing barriers to success in the community. RPUMC works closely with leaders from the City of Tukwila and the Tukwila School District in identifying areas of need in the community.

Discussion Questions

Chapter 8: God Saw It and It Was Good
By Rev. Jan Bolerjack

What are some creative ways that church can be financially sustainable in communities that cannot afford to pay staff?

Mental illness, addiction, and homelessness are often intertwined. Are there ministries effectively dealing with this issue?

CHAPTER NINE

Holy Conversation:
One Beer at a Time

By Rev. Emma Donohew

For where two or three are gathered in my name,
I am there among them."

Matthew 18-20 (NSRV)

I can remember sitting alone at a table in a basement pub
on a rainy Pacific Northwest evening, a few questions scrib-
bled on sticky notes, wondering if anyone would show up.
I was serving my first church at quarter time (ten hours a
week) and I was determined to start something new for people
who were seeking good conversation around diverse topics. So,
I invited people to a pub to talk about God, over a beer, because
that's not awkward, right? Especially in a region known for its
aversion to organized religion. However, I was determined to
give Pub Theology a try no matter what, so after a few tense
minutes, people not only began to show up, but they shared,
conversed, and created community in the most sacred of ways
unlike anything I had experienced in my church life so far.

In cities throughout the Pacific Northwest, it's easier to
invite someone to a bar, brewery, or coffee shop than it is to
invite someone to church. This is because sometimes our
spaces can be a barrier to those who might find entering
a church daunting. People don't come to church for many
reasons, so I figured I could either wait for people to come to

me/the church, or I could answer the Great Commission, and go to where the people are.

In Seattle, a city home to sixty breweries and counting (that's just in the city limits), beer is its own category of conversation. People will speak passionately about their favorite fresh hop beer, or if barrel-aged beer has gone too far or not far enough. If you can get past the local craft beer list however, people are hungry for deeper conversation. This isn't just unique to Seattle, but to communities throughout the Pacific Northwest. I think that the church is a place that can offer this if we are willing to go where the people are.

Facilitating Pub Theology conversations from Bellingham and Seattle, Washington to Portland, Oregon has taught me a lot about what the people of the None Zone are seeking.

- Community

- Gathering Places

- Conversations

- And Beer (or cider, or coffee, or niche beverage of your choosing).

I know this because I was and always will be seeking it as well. The Pacific Northwest is a place of strong palates, opinions, and feelings, and not enough outlets to share them. The church can be that outlet. Sometimes we just need places that feel a little less like church for it to truly become a holy outlet, and dare I say, a sacred space.

So, we started meeting in pubs, breweries, and bars, inviting people to come together around a table sharing their values, feelings, and questions around themes and topics that are often off limits in other areas of life.

Experience has taught me that the key to a well-guided

Pub Theology conversation is to allow the questions to guide you, with no intended outcome. Theology is the study of how we talk about God, so why confine the conversation with limitations before you even begin. All topics must be accessible and all types of people of faith and no faith must be welcome.

From death and mortality, consumerism, reproductive rights, online dating, doubt, climate change, compassion fatigue, money, and more, these are the topics you were warned to avoid at the dinner table. Which is exactly why we need to be talking about them and framing these conversations in a way that includes spirituality and faith as a lens. We are called to not only help people find their voice but use it. Pub Theology is a space for people to gather, discuss, pray, doodle, and actively participate in the world around them; the world not separate from God, but deeply infused with God.

In Portland after a conversation on death, we shared ashes in the sign of the cross, from our Ash Wednesday service, with thirty of those gathered in a crowded restaurant. As we reflected on our mortality, with ashen faces, the kitchen staff invited us back to impose ashes and pray with each of their staff members who had not been able to make it to church. Yes, it was an unusual setting, but God showed up. Especially in those unexpected places, when we share our faith and God's love humbly, and compassionately, with one another and the world.

The church, even from founding was never meant to be contained to one building. Jesus specified gathering in his name, but never specified where. Now more than ever, it is up to the church to facilitate sacred space both in and outside of its walls. Inevitably in the process of sharing something that brings you joy with others, people and a faithful community will gather and evolve, in Jesus' name, if we let it.

This is how theology is done: Around tables. Over beers. Sharing our hearts. Finding God's love. Communicating honestly and compassionately.

Inspired by the message of Jesus and his action of spending more time outside the temple than in it, and more time around a table, than behind a pulpit, I have continued to let the spirit guide me as I find creative avenues like Pub Theology to answer the Great Commission. The gospel of love knows no boundaries! The gospel of hope knows no limits. The gospel of truth knows nothing is off limits.

Churches should be a place where everyone can be honest and we can tell our truths, but sometimes this doesn't happen because people are afraid of what others might think of their beliefs or even their doubts about religion or faith.

People need a place to wrestle with big ideas, and I believe the church providing as many avenues as possible for this to happen, is following in the footsteps of Jesus. Where we meet matters, and utilizing the spaces we have been given is crucial, so in a region full of well-crafted watering holes, why not utilize some of these other God-given spaces to do fruitful ministry?

As Benjamin Franklin was rumored to have said, "Beer is proof that God loves us, and wants us to be happy." Why not create more spaces and opportunities for people to find out that God loves them and wants them to be happy and spiritually engaged too, no matter where we are or what we are drinking?

God calls us around many tables throughout our lives, because the table is the place where theology is done. Since Pub Theology is still church, we end each of my gatherings with prayer. It's amazing to see Christians, atheists, agnostics, and people of other faiths, say first with hesitancy, and then with certainty, "I guess, I do have a prayer."

Our best Christian witness in the world is civil dialogue and compassionate listening. When we do those things, God shows up and does more than we can imagine. So, find God's people spread throughout your community, at your local coffee shops, watering holes, breweries, pubs, and restaurants and invite them to chat over your favorite beverage. God will meet you there.

Emma Donohew is a pastor in the Pacific Northwest, having served Green Lake and Crown Hill United Methodist Churches in Seattle and Parkrose United Methodist Church in Portland, Oregon. Currently she is living and working in Bellingham, Washington. Inspired by her Methodist roots of taking the church beyond the building, she has facilitated a weekly Pub Theology conversation for the past six years to foster questions, not quarrels.

She attended University of Puget Sound and received her Master of Divinity from Pacific School of Religion, in Berkeley, CA, studying the intersection between art and religion. When she's not creating art or encouraging others to do the same, she can be found crafting cider with her husband Eric or hiking in the mountains with their hound dog, Molly.

Discussion Questions

Chapter 9:
Holy Conversation: One Beer at a Time
By Rev. Emma Donohew

What would it take to have sacred conversations in the public spaces in your community?

What is different about sacred conversation in church and sacred conversation in a public space?

CHAPTER TEN

Gathered and Sent

Rev. Joseph D. Kim

[6] For this reason I remind you to rekindle the gift of God that is within you through the laying on of my hands; [7] for God did not give us a spirit of cowardice, but rather a spirit of power and of love and of self-discipline.

– 2 Timothy 1:6-7 (NRSV)

I was in my first semester of seminary sitting in my Early and Medieval Church History course. I had just left a comfortable church bureaucracy position in Washington, DC, with lofty and idealistic dreams of being with the people, making a difference, changing lives. To me, that meant following in the footsteps of generations before me and becoming a pastor of a local church.

Hence, there I was in my first week of classes, sitting on the left side about halfway back in the auditorium where Professor Paul Rorem[7] was introducing the course. One of the very first things he said was that despite all its diversity, church history did have a center, and he argued that the church has always been, and continues to be, defined as *Biblical communities of worship, gathered and sent – Biblical Communities* as in communities rooted in the legacy and stories of the Bible, *Worship* as in giving glory to God, *Gathered* as in coming

---

7   Benjamin B. Warfield Professor of Medieval Church History at Princeton Theological Seminary

together, *Sent* as in going out.

Fast-forward and now, I have the joy and privilege of being the lead pastor of Bothell United Methodist Church, a church in a northern suburb of Seattle, where close to 400 people gather on a Sunday morning as we equip ourselves and one another in our purpose of *Becoming Christ in the Community*. We believe that we are partnering alongside what God is already doing, and we work towards our goals of

- Transformed People

- Transformed Relationships

- Transformed Conditions.

It's easy to list off the ways we are living into the "sent" part of Dr. Rorem's definition of church. We send teams to the Democratic Republic of the Congo where we partner with two local orphanages. We commission teams to Salt Lake City where the United Methodist Church Committee on Relief (UMCOR) has one of their relief supply depots assembling kits to be sent to places in need of humanitarian relief. We partner with other local churches and community leaders supporting those who are homeless, through winter shelters, transitional housing, and advocacy on behalf of individuals. We host a free community meal called Bothell Community Kitchen every Sunday evening for anyone in the community to share in food and friendship – and we have yet to miss a Sunday since its start in 2009.

If we're honest, the "sent" or "sending" of the church is easy, especially for those of us who claim the high-achieving busy-ness and identity of liberal and progressive Seattle as our own. We're conditioned to place value and priority in the doing, busying ourselves with tasks, particularly tasks that help people, and we do our best to make a difference in the world. So, "sent?" Without question. But, "gathered?"

We're reminded that we live in the None Zone – the region of the United States characterized by the growing population of those who identify as "nones" and "dones." We're told that the "nones" – religiously non-affiliated Americans – make up nearly a quarter of the overall population and a full third of Americans under the age of thirty. And "dones" refer to a subgroup of "nones" who were once religiously affiliated but have no interest of ever affiliating again. They're not just unaffiliated, they are anti-affiliated.[8]

In April 2018, Gallup released poll data on faith in America, and in it, Washington was ranked among the least religious states in the country. In fact, according to Gallup, Washington was the sixth-least-religious state in the country with 47 percent of adults saying they are not religious and seldom or never attend services.[9]

And yet, we at Bothell United Methodist Church choose to gather. We make the conscious decision to gather. We gather at three distinct services on Sunday morning – a contemplative, a traditional, and a contemporary – with programming for children and youth, and we gather when we don't have to. We gather, because there's power in gathering.

I remember one Sunday evening during that time of the year when it wasn't quite spring, but not yet summer, and

8 Carter, N. "The "Nones" vs. the "Dones". Patheos.com (blog), March 27, 2015. https://www.patheos.com/blogs/godlessindixie/2015/03/27/the-nones-vs-the-dones/ #riwKqc5Yu8R1RvEd.99/

9 Balk, G. "Washingtonians are less religious than ever, Gallup poll finds." *The Seattle Times*, April 20, 2018. https://www.seattletimes.com/seattle-news/data/ washingtonians-are-less-religious-than-ever-gallup-poll-finds/

our children's music ministry had just wrapped up another successful year of programming. Three separate children's choirs, countless parents and adult volunteers, and joy and a passion for music-making – all reasons to celebrate and we held a potluck-style gathering at church.

As potlucks go, it wasn't anything out of the ordinary. There was the usual assortment of burgers, salads, and casseroles galore, and the choir leaders, the children, and their parents spent the evening reflecting upon and sharing in the joys of the program year.

As the potluck came to an end and after all was cleaned up, I noticed that the families were not leaving. Instead, they moved their conversations outside the building and into the parking lot. And then they stayed there for two full hours talking and laughing and sharing in life together.

There's something to sharing life together, to doing life together, that excites me about church, but more than that, it's the *desire* to gather that brings me hope.

Since 2016, we have been tweaking the opportunities provided for spiritual formation and community building. At the time, we had somewhere close to eighty people participating in some kind of study, small group, or form of faith development. In 2017, we doubled involvement to 160 people. This year, in 2018, we registered 250 people who named that they wanted to be intentional in gathering. There's a group that meets every Wednesday morning for Bible Study and a group that experiences God in their monthly hikes together. There is a group doing yoga together every week, and a group connecting through flutes. A group that meets monthly for dinner and conversation, and a group that gathers to be creative and make art.

In one such group, there was a man who was diagnosed

with cancer, who told me that because of my age and lack of life-experience, I would never know what he was and would be going through. And he was right. I promised to pray for him and sent him on his way, only to find out that the members of his group were providing abundant loving care for him – they prayed for him and with him, they cooked the kind of meals that he was allowed to eat on his new diet, they sat with him so that his wife could have a few hours to herself in her garden without worrying about him, and after he died, they helped his widow pack boxes and clean, and eventually sell the house.

These groups commit to being with one another, to care for one another, to pray for one another, to grow together, and that is a powerful thing. When everything in society tells us to be afraid and to isolate ourselves because that is the way we are going to get ahead, instead we gather, becoming vulnerable with one another and sharing in life.

Everything about this – about doing life together – is counter-cultural, I think. From willingly gathering with one another throughout the week when we could be prioritizing work or homework or an extracurricular activity to choosing to be present on Sunday morning, I'm grateful to be serving a congregation that has not bought into a message of doom and gloom of church decline. We are not ashamed to do church, to be church, to be people *gathered* in love and *sent* for trans-formation. We are not ashamed to challenge the values of our society, the values of our American, capitalistic, consumeris-tic, dog-eat-dog, love is weak, and vulnerability is bad society; the one that tells us to be only thinking about the me, the I, to put myself ahead of and above the rest.

Every time we gather at church, whether throughout the week or on a Sunday morning, we are reminded of this core identity, of being people *gathered and sent*, of being people who challenge the notion that we are to be separate and apart, fear-ing the other, isolated and doing life alone.

On banners at every entrance of our building, on the cover of all our weekly bulletins, out of the mouths of our clergy at the start of every worship service, we say the words of our Welcome Statement:

> Bothell United Methodist Church affirms that God's grace and peace are freely given to everyone. God's gifts are not limited by a person's economic means, health, or social condition. Our hearts, minds, and doors are always open to people of all ages, abilities, races, nationalities, sexual orientations, gender identities, and marital status.
>
> We invite you to join us as we strive to live out our purpose of "Becoming Christ in the Community." With God's guidance and strength, we can transform the world. Wherever you are on your spiritual journey, know that you are welcome here.

When today's cultural and political climate cannot affirm the simple truth that *God's grace and peace are freely given to everyone,* when even places that claim to be sacred cannot affirm that simple truth, we buy into the false sense of comfort that is brought forth through isolation. We build walls to propel us towards individual success or in the aspirations of success, or walls to protect ourselves from fear of the other or what is different, or even walls of indifference.

But when we gather, we affirm that God's grace and peace **are** freely given to everyone, that all are welcome wherever one is on their spiritual journey.

I don't know what Christianity in the Pacific Northwest will look like in the next one, five, ten, fifty years – what form it will take, what messages it will send, what places it will call home, who will even claim it as their own. The trends seem to point to some blend of post-modern Christianity, placing value in orthopraxy (right practice) over orthodoxy (right belief). But one thing is certain, the church of that future Christianity in the Pacific Northwest will continue to challenge isolation and division. We will still *gather,* and we will still be *sent.* And in that, I find power and hope – it's the essence of who we are, who we are called to be.

I remember attending a conference where the keynote speaker was sharing a presentation on effective ministry leadership. To a room of both clergy and lay people, he invited us to look around the room and proceeded to ask us if anyone else in the room had seen the inside of our refrigerator at home. The room began to chuckle as he continued. If someone has not seen the inside of your refrigerator, that person is not your friend, that person is your colleague. The point he was making was to have clear boundaries and to set realistic expectations in the relationships we have in ministry. There will be some that are friends, there will be many that are colleagues. The key, he argued, is to know the difference and to honor those relationships as they really are, not what we pretend them to be.

I was incredibly challenged by this, though, probably not in the way he intended. If I claimed the foundation of my ministry to be in the gathering and sending of people, if this was the model of ministry that would transform people, transform relationships, and transform conditions, then how come most of the community at Bothell United Methodist Church has never seen the inside of my refrigerator?

Since then, we have gathered not just at church but in our homes, the places where we are vulnerable. Joann and I hosted the training for small group leaders, youth visioning, and planning sessions, and we have had four different Christmas parties over two weeks to thank and celebrate the amazing teams that make ministries happen at our church.

Now, many ministries at Bothell United Methodist Church gather in homes, often starting with food and fellowship, before attending to the business at hand. Sometimes, food and fellowship are the business at hand. You see, every time we come together, for whatever reason, something amazing happens. The walls we have literally built around our houses come down, and the walls we have built around our hearts fall away. We share in life and we share in love.

It was at one of these gatherings where I ran into long-time church goer, T. T is unique. He is an older, very White man, who sits by himself in the back of our worship space, seemingly uninterested in the service. But every time he comes to receive the bread during communion, week after week, he always responds, "gracias."

I believe that it was because walls were broken that I finally worked up the courage to ask him why he responded in Spanish. He said, there was a time when he hated immigrants, especially Spanish-speaking immigrants. He lived in a part of town that was being "overrun" by them and he hated them for taking jobs, for making his town dirty, for being different. One day, while praying, he felt God break him and his heart, and he committed to learning Spanish so that he could be neighbors to them and eventually friends. After hearing this, I couldn't help but cry. I now give him the bread speaking Spanish, "El cuerpo del Jesus Christo para ti." And he responds, "gracias."

When we gather, when we share in love, and when we choose to do life together, transformation happens. May our lives be agents of transformation, that the power in gathering would send us to live our purpose of *becoming Christ in the community.*

Rev. Joseph D. Kim serves as the lead pastor of Bothell United Methodist Church. He has served at Salem United Methodist Church in Harlem, New York. Before entering parish ministry, Joe was the Director of Children's Rights Advocacy at the General Board of Church and Society of the United Methodist Church in Washington, D.C., where he focused on policy and advocacy efforts to combat human trafficking and promote equal education opportunities for all children. He has also served as Director for Community Care at Spark12, Senior Associate for Membership Development and Services for the Conference of Non-Governmental Organizations in Consultative Relationship with the United Nations, and Program and Administrative Assistant at the General Board of Church and Society of the United Methodist Church, United Nations Office. He has traveled around the world as a speaker, workshop leader and facilitator, encouraging people of faith to do justice, to love kindness, and to walk humbly with God.

He has studied at the University of Michigan (B.A. in English and Political Science 2007), Princeton Theological Seminary, and Claremont School of Theology (M.Div. 2017).

Joe is the husband to an incredibly talented artist and justice-seeker, Joann, dad to two fun-loving children, son Asher and daughter Ember, and best friend to their dog, Leigh. Joe loves being outdoors, traveling, and enjoys all things music and sports.

Discussion Questions

Chapter 10:
Gathered and Sent

By Rev. Joe Kim

Which resonates with you: gathering or sending?

What is important about gathering?

How is gathering counter-cultural?

CHAPTER Eleven

Holding Tight to a Grinning God

By Rev. Jenny Smith

*Remain in me, and I will remain in you. A branch can't produce
fruit by itself, but must remain in the vine. Likewise, you
can't produce fruit unless you remain in me. I am the vine; you
are the branches. If you remain in me and I in you, then you
will produce much fruit. Without me, you can't do anything.*

– John 15:4-5 (CEB)[10]

"I didn't know a place like this existed."

A soft smile sneaks onto my face. "It's fascinating, isn't it?"

This exchange has happened in coffee shops, church
offices, hallways, and by email more times than I can count.
I'm still surprised that people are surprised when they stum-
ble across an inclusive faith community that places God's
grace at the center of all they do.

We talk often in Marysville, Washington about our call to
tell a different kind of faith story. The church has taken this so
seriously that they created and affirmed this statement back
in 2015. We've been living it out ever since with grace, humility, and a fair number of mistakes.

We commit ourselves to the hospitality Jesus taught, by creat-

---

10 *Common English Bible (CEB)*, 2011 by Common English Bible

ing a place of safety and spiritual sanctuary for all people. We welcome into full participation in the life of this church people of every race, ethnicity, age, ability, physical or mental condition, socioeconomic status, political affiliation, gender identity, sexual orientation, and family structure.

By the way, sexual orientation used to be the element we were most mindful of. But now? Welcoming all, regardless of political affiliation, is challenging each of us to see those with whom we disagree as a child of God.

Kate was a thirty-three-year-old woman who nervously entered our doors a couple years ago. She'd combed through our website and wondered if everything she'd read would be true in person. I received an email after her first visit that confirmed she had found something unique and meaningful. After several important but tense faith environments, a community centered on true inclusion and grace was like a clear stream of water in the desert.

We met, and I shared with her the contemplative stance we learned from Dr. Elaine Heath that inspired our way of being:

Show Up, Pay Attention, Cooperate with God, and Release the Outcome.

This rhythm has brought deep transformation, powerful community, and a joy that's palpable. Guests often comment on the energy in the atmosphere, even when they step into the empty building. God is up to something in these people and it's an honor to steward this energy and make room for God to lead.

I sensed something in Kate that first day we met. Like us all, God had something for her to do in this world and I wondered if our faith community would be a part of it.

I've spent most of my ministry trying to figure out vision.

How does a church catch a vision? Does a pastor go to the mountaintop and come down with a vision like Moses or is it birthed in community? How do we best lead our churches so our work really matters? I've got one life to live and I don't want to waste time playing church. From day one in this appointment, I've been praying and looking and wondering and listening for vision.

Crickets.

I've pleaded, begged, cried, and looked everywhere for what important thing God wanted to do with us.

We knew the basics. We would love people with abandon. We would meet needs where we could and be a part of larger conversations about why the need existed in the first place. We would laugh together and share the parts of ourselves that were too often hidden behind the Sunday morning conversation, "I'm fine. Things are good." But part of me always felt invited into something more than I could see at the time.

One sunny August afternoon, I got into my car to head home. Something nudged me to drive out the back driveway of the church. My attention was drawn to one of my favorite trees. The sun was shining through the green leaves as they fluttered in the light breeze. I pulled over, parked, and walked over to the tree. Standing at the bottom, I gazed up at the leaves.

A very strong awareness suddenly washed over me. God was the tree. My job was to hold tight to this tree trunk. I was to stay connected to God as a source of strength and steady calm in this season. My eyes almost bore holes through this tree as I memorized how it felt to stay connected. Then God lifted my gaze heavenward and I saw countless leaves in every direction. The leaves became people and names and stories that were coming to life. They were beautiful! I felt God whisper, "Child, stay connected to me and people will come to know me, and you might not even know their name."

Remain in me, and I will remain in you. A branch can't produce fruit by itself but must remain in the vine.

Part of our journey as a church has been about seeing something new that we couldn't see before.

Chris and Nichole enrolled their daughter in our preschool. They got to know a few people in the church and started asking questions. One conversation led to another and one question led to lots more questions. The love of this community carried them along to a decision to get baptized and become a part of these people. Chris has served on our leadership team and Nichole now serves as our Director of Welcoming Ministries. Their questions and curiosity about God have enlivened the relationships of many who had come to take their faith for granted.

Karen leaned on a walker as she quietly whispered in my ear, "Pastor, I'm ready to get baptized." Karen had been a part of our community for several months and a painful story has emerged as she's trusted us more and more. For the longest time, Karen wore dark-colored hoodies. They felt safe in her unsafe world.

Over time, Karen started wearing light-colored hoodies. When asked about it, she shared, "I used to come here just to come. It was something to do. But now, I want to be here. I want to be a part of everything. I feel safe. I feel loved." One day, maybe the hoodie will come off.

Speaking of people seeing new things, this even extends to their pastor. I've battled with anxiety and panic attacks much of my adult life. There is a low-grade anxiety for many of us in today's world that constantly pulls us out of the present moment and into a fear of what could be. When I started to have panic attacks while preaching, I knew this was different.

I decided to pull back the covers on my life and shine a light on what I was so afraid of. It began a life-changing journey into my fear. When the time came to share this with my faith community, their love and grace took my breath away.

I had a panic attack in the middle of a sermon and for the first time I stopped and told my church. This happened in our traditional service and I was nervous they wouldn't understand. But to my surprise, they stood up, gathered around me, and prayed. After everyone sat down, I smiled through my tears and said I wasn't sure whether to finish my sermon or not. An eighty-two-year-old in the second row piped up, "we already had our sermon for today."

So when someone asks what's special about this faith community, what do I say? The level of authenticity and sharing that's invited into this space is transformational. God's spirit sits at the center of this community and welcomes all kinds of mess and pain and truth. From that space, people are invited into an adventure they could never travel alone.

Remember my moment with the tree in the backyard? I hope no one was watching as I all but hugged that tree. Our prayer and listening for vision continued that fall. We arrived at our charge conference at the end of November and I was experiencing a quiet shift. I was done trying to figure it out.

A peace descended as I stood up before our people and invited them to pray together that Advent season. Our prayer: *God, we are yours. What do you want to do through us?* Ironically, it was a prayer of desperation. I threw it out there and didn't really think they'd do it. Isn't that awful?! Sometimes we pastors don't trust our people nearly enough. But they were listening. A week later, multiple people shared how the prayer was affecting them. I realized I'd better get on board!

I set aside time each morning during Advent to lift those

words to God. All these things started to move inside me. Things I had always said no to now sounded like intriguing ideas. Places where I had experienced resistance became soft and pliable. In the next few weeks, a vision would emerge that after being discerned with multiple groups, rose to the surface of who we would become next.

What if we birthed ten new expressions of church in the next thirty years?

By 2030, we see ten communities of faith thriving in our county. They are vibrant and alive. Each community has a deep sense of grace and love for all people. Each one looks different. For all our friends who might never enter the door of a building like ours, what if church looked differently than we thought it could? Some might be clergy-led while others might be lay-led. Some are deeply connected in relationship with Marysville United Methodist Church. Others may be chartered as a church out on their own. They are all encouraged and loved by the people of Marysville United Methodist Church. The new expressions are collaborative, contextual, and grounded in a discipleship rhythm of showing up, paying attention, cooperating with God, and releasing the outcome.

A long line of pastors had done incredible work so this church could be healthy. Our finances were in order, our building was cared for, and we shifted our leadership structure to a single board to better discern our work in the world. These beloved people clothed kids, rebuilt homes after wildfires, fed the hungry, listened to the depressed, gave prayer quilts to the ill, and made sure families were supported. This church was healthy and alive. We had a responsibility and opportunity to become healthy soil for new expressions of church to come into existence.

I mentioned Kate earlier. She eventually became our Director of Family Ministries and thrived in bringing love to life for our kids and families. As this ten in thirty vision emerged, we learned our conference leaders were assessing people to be church planters. They asked if Kate wanted to enter that process. Turns out God built Kate to be a church planter too! She has incredible gifts for connecting with people who aren't so sure about the church or God. And our leaders wanted Kate to lead our first new expression! We couldn't believe it. She took time to think on it and visions started to flow out of her for what might be possible. Kate saw something new and was willing to be used by God.

So that's where we're at today. We have a crazy idea and a person who's ready to be the midwife. We have a healthy church who sees their joy and responsibility to be healthy soil for other communities to grow. We get to keep being who we are in the world. I get to keep clinging to the tree and trusting God is guiding this thing.

We're in the awkward part of the journey where we can't quite see what's next. But we know God is at work. We get to cooperate and release the outcome. We've been training for this for years.

Someone asked me recently, "What will you do if some of these communities don't work out?" This is the gift of serving in the None Zone. There's really no such thing as failure. Everything is an experiment because we're living in a reality that seminary couldn't prepare us for. We will learn, let things die, and start again whenever needed. It's freeing to know we can't fail.

We often talk about how God has this irritating way of illuminating steps one and two, but not three and four. As a community, we're starting to trust this truth. Our job is to live in the tension of seeing part of the image, but not the whole thing. And maybe it's learning this that helps us dream bigger dreams for our communities. To step into a wild adventure with God, we have to let go of so many certainties. This is tough but necessary work.

Eight months into our time in Marysville, I was lying down to sleep one night and feeling out of sorts. I thought, "Jesus, give me something." The next thought that popped into my head surprised me. I saw God holding a blanket to cover a big painting. God kept looking at me and then back at the painting. At me and back at the painting. God was grinning! Then God said, "My child, it's about to get even better."

When I was seventeen, I stood in a room full of teenagers also exploring a call into ordained ministry in the United Methodist Church. I knew, without a shadow of a doubt, this was my calling. God designed me to be a pastor. I was called to love people, love God, and help them meet each other.

If you had turned to me and said, "Hey, one day you're going to help make room for ten new expressions of church to emerge in a place where most people don't like church," I would have rolled my eyes and walked away.

I never would have thought this grinning God had dreams like this in store for the Pacific Northwest, a place where so many roll their eyes at the God they know.

The best part about living in the None Zone is it feels like no one is obligated to gather as the body of Christ. Culture doesn't encourage it as a spoken or unspoken expectation. So when I stand up on a Sunday morning and gaze out upon thirsty, tired, and beautiful people, I know they *want* to be there. No one would be surprised if they chose Sunday morning brunch by the water or stayed in bed and watched Netflix. But instead, each of these people chose (well, except maybe some of those teenagers) to make their way to a building to hear again of a love that erases every boundary they tried to create that week. They squeeze the hand of a loved one after harsh words on Friday night as if to say, "Let's start over." Someone stands to offer a story of how the love of God is changing the way they see a tough relationship. They speak up for someone who doesn't have a voice. They offer a gift so that someone gets a new home after a wildfire or gently used clothes for school. Their shaky but determined voices join the people around them as music is placed on the altar of God.

This is the body of Christ. It is beautiful to behold. And God is grinning.

Rev. Jenny Smith grew up in Ohio and Alaska. She is a 2005 graduate of Florida Southern College and a 2010 graduate of United Theological Seminary. Jenny was ordained an elder in the Pacific Northwest Conference in 2012. She served two appointments in the Alaska Conference before moving to Marysville in 2015. Jenny is married to Aaron and they have two children, Isabella and Wesley.

Discussion Questions

Chapter 11:
Holding Tight to a Grinning God
By Rev. Jenny Smith

If you were to create a "new expression of church," what would it look like?

What does it mean that a church could be "contextual?"

What does it take to "release the outcome" of an idea?

CHAPTER TWELVE

To Reach the Nones and Dones, Focus on the Ones

By Rev. Jeremy Smith

[8] The one who plants and the one who waters work together, but each one will receive their own reward for their own labor. [9] We are God's coworkers, and you are God's field, God's building.

– 1 Corinthians 3:8-9 (CEB)[11]

Bible Belt Eyes in the Pacific Northwest

I'm a transplant to the Pacific Northwest, having been raised in the Bible Belt and pastorally-trained on the East Coast. After serving two churches in Massachusetts and Oklahoma, I found my theological home in the urban Northwest. As of this publication date, I will have pastored for seven years at downtown churches in Portland, Oregon and Seattle, Washington.

I moved to the Pacific Northwest a few years after Amy Frykholm wrote about it as "The None Zone" in Christian Century's December 2008 edition. That was the first article I read when I learned of my new placement. I was enamored with the term, wanting to hold this people group in my hands and understand the contours of them, asking, "What happened to you that would cause you to choose an unaffiliated life?"

But a funny thing happened on the way to the Nones. I ran into the Dones.

---

11 *Common English Bible (CEB)*, 2011 by Common English Bible

And then after the Dones, I ran into the Ones.

And that's when things really started getting interesting.

Because I found out that for all the churches fretting about the Nones and the Dones, I believe real transformation can come when churches focus on the Ones.

The Nones and Dones

Over the past few years, experts on religious studies have written about two groups who are negatively affecting religious adherence rates in America.

The first is the "Nones," the increasing number of Americans who check "none" on the religious affiliation section of polls and census forms. This does not mean they are atheist/ freethinking (though some are). It means they do not identify with any religion. This number is highest in the Pacific Northwest and pockets of the Northeast. Other authors in this book have wrestled with this term better than I, so I won't rehash the definition.

The second are the "Dones," the folks who are done with church. Authors Ashleigh Hope and Josh Packard in their book, *Church Refugees*, define "Dones" as a wholly different kind of churchgoer. They are:

> "[P]eople who make explicit and intentional decisions to leave the church and organized religion. We call these people the de-churched or the Dones. They're done with church. They're tired and fed up with church. They're dissatisfied with the structure, social message, and politics of the institutional church, and they've decided they and their spiritual lives are better off lived outside of organized religion."

"Dones" identify as Christian but due to church politics, lack of hospitality, toxic culture against LGBTQIA+ persons, or a myriad of other reasons, have decided to walk away and not affiliate. In a culture without a dominant religious group like the Pacific Northwest, I've met a lot of "Dones" who feel more latitude to disaffiliate rather than optimistically church-hop to the next steeple.

Reams of paper have been printed and billions of pixels have been lit up with analysis and advice of how to deal with these two phenomena. There are particular churches, ministries, and missions that appeal to Nones and Dones with success, and I'm thankful for them.

However, my experience leads me to believe that most churches would do better to focus on a third group: the Ones.

...and the Ones

At the risk of arbitrarily and sloppily creating a new people group, the Ones are folks who adhere to a church (not a None), and attend that church (not a Done), but participate in only ONE activity in that faith community.

For most churches, the Ones are folks who only attend worship services and otherwise do not participate in other parts of the church. The best of them worship once a week, give a tithe, welcome visitors, and usher or assist with that worship service in some way. They may participate fully in that one activity, but they do not regularly participate in any other aspect of the church, such as Sunday school classes, service events, or even social outings.

While found throughout Christendom, in the Pacific Northwest the Ones have a special quality. There are high number of Ones who are connected with the church solely through one of its outreach or community offerings. There are folks who only attend a Sunday school class, who only attend particular service opportunities, and who only attend events that reflect their age group or people group. Their "one" thing often isn't a worship service. It's another aspect of the faith community. To be fair, they attend or volunteer faithfully!

Ones do one thing, and often do it well.

But as their resident theologian and pastor, Ones are problematic for me.

One Activity, One Experience

Often, the Ones are appreciated by pastors, but for the wrong reasons. They attend and are members, often tithe, but don't participate elsewhere in the church. They give a "plus one" to the two statistics that are most looked at by external evaluators (attendance and membership), and they often passively accept whatever the church does.

But I believe we are doing people a spiritual disservice when we allow them to stay in their one activity for years on end.

When people participate in two aspects of a faith community, they are able to bring different parts of themselves to their spirituality. It's not just a difference between experiencing broadcast spirituality (sermon) and interactive spirituality (education, service, witness). Rather, they are able to apply their faith in a different context, which makes it easier to apply their faith in secular contexts. Even for those who attend service events and not worship, imagine how fulfilling their service would be with the week's message or a Sunday school topic as a conversation starter with a fellow volunteer.

Interdisciplinary learning is a prerequisite of many secular companies. Why isn't inter-ministry experience an expectation of faith traditions?

To be clear, there are certain folks who are justifiably Ones. The very elderly and those with disabilities often participate in worship and maybe a handful of other events each year. That's fine and they are not the focus of this conversation. Though, I always tell them if they can receive prayer requests by phone or letter, they can join the Prayer Team. Then, they ARE involved in worship ... plus one.

A Volunteer, Plus One

Expecting additional volunteering should be easy. Rates of volunteerism in the urban Pacific Northwest are higher than the national average according to the Corporation for National & Community Service website. It should be easy to encourage folks to volunteer both at church and at a community service opportunity or education experience.

But wait. The second activity has to be inside the church, part of the church's mission, ministry, and outreach. Why is that? Why can't the "plus one" activity be with a community service group outside of the church? Can I be a Scout leader, or be on the board of a non-profit? Why does it have to be a group within the church?

Let me use the church I serve as an example. First United Methodist Church in downtown Seattle has a Shared Breakfast that is served every Sunday to those experiencing hunger and homelessness in downtown Seattle. In 2018, they served over 16,000 meals, rotating teams of volunteers serving over 300 guests each Sunday. It is not a "hear a sermon then get a meal" manipulative witness. It is simply a warm plate and a smiling server, along with resources offered and physical needs met. There are many volunteers who do the dishes, cook eggs, or serve in some way.

One volunteer in particular started attending worship in recent months after I kept up a running weekly conversation with him, adding a "plus one" to his involvement. One Sunday, I caught him explaining the sermon to several guys experiencing homelessness on the street later that day. What better bearer of the bread of life than one who they just saw serving bread earlier that day? How could that moment have been replicated by volunteering with another organization instead of colliding service with worship, perspiration with inspiration? It could, but I believe digging deeper into one's faith requires looking from multiple perspectives, turning a gem in the light and see what reflects differently. As Paul reminds us in 1 Corinthians, we are blessed according to the labor that we do. How much more blessed would we be when we bring two labors together?

While the volunteer benefited from experiencing two different parts of church, I would caution that you can't be heavy-handed with the hope for everyone. Some volunteers have their own places of worship or philosophical practices, and that's terrific. Being overbearing with invitations can drive them from that One involvement! Committing to being a presence with and alongside folks as they navigate their own spiritual experiences, I believe brings a more holistic reward than simply volunteering with many different organizations. The depth and breadth of which sustains a healthy volunteer ethic for wherever the volunteer finds themselves.

How Do We Reach the Ones?

Imagine if everyone in your pews was involved in ONE other part of the church on a regular, intentional basis. What transformation might take place beyond more people in service to more involvement in discipling practices?

I'm from the Bible Belt, which has an obsession with numbers and quantifiable results. The Pacific Northwest generally doesn't have that philosophy, so it is nice in this case that I actually have hard data to respond to this question.

The Rev. Jenny Smith, a fellow author in this book, shared with me how her previous church in Alaska ministered with the Ones. St. John United Methodist Church in Anchorage began a Worship+ intentional process. They wanted church members to be in worship plus at least one other activity in their faith community. Among other things, they began offering a dedicated "discipleship hour" on Sundays with a variety of offerings (not just Sunday school classes). After a year of Worship+, they discovered three things:

- All their Sunday morning extra experiences (education and service opportunities) were led by their laity, not their clergy.

- Previously, they had thirty adults participate in Sunday school. After the Worship+ initiative, they had 150 adults participating in the variety of offerings in that same time slot.

- They experienced an overall increase in children and youth participation, although they ended up participating at times other than Sunday morning. Families dedicating over two hours on Sundays was difficult!

First United Methodist Church in Portland is another example. When I was on staff there, we began intentional efforts to get fifty percent of the congregation involved in a small group. When we began the three-year project, about twenty-seven percent of the church was involved in a small group, but some of those groups were longtime social gatherings, closed to outsiders. By doing intentional coordination and similar values-sharing of "we want you in worship AND any of our small groups," within three years we crossed the fifty-one percent threshold, and all the small groups were open to newcomers. Both of these are mainline churches in

The None Zone that should be declining, but instead have experienced an increase in discipleship among the people already participating. It has led to numerical growth as well as an increased number of people who are applying their spirituality in different ways, both in sacred and secular spaces.

Calling the Ones to Become Twos

In conclusion, when I was applying to seminary, my entrance essay was about how The Great Commission was about discipleship, not evangelism. When Jesus said in Matthew 28 to "make disciples of all nations," He didn't say "make Christians of all nations." Discipleship is more than believers and members of churches. I think discipleship means to enter into the types of situations where our faith is applied, and I believe that happens best when we participate in more than *one* aspect of the church.

When the Ones become the Twos, the math doesn't work out because they often experience exponential growth in their applied spirituality. For this reason, I firmly believe raising the bar for discipleship will be better for everyone. No matter how high or low a commitment that Plus One activity is, it opens up a space where transformation happens.

The winnowing of the church is ahead of us, and in the Pacific Northwest it has already begun. I believe discipleship that transforms the Ones into Twos will carry us through our present time, a discipleship that leads to an evangelical spirit of bringing our faith with us to acts of service, efforts towards justice, and community betterment. May we know that all are called to this witness in whatever corner of the world you are in.[12]

---

12 Hope, Ashleigh, and Packard, Josh Ph.D. Church Refugees. Loveland: Group Publishing, 2015.

The Rev. Jeremy Smith is Senior Pastor of First United Methodist Church of Seattle, the oldest church of any denomination in the city. Previously, Jeremy has pastored churches in Oregon, Oklahoma, and Massachusetts.

Jeremy is best known for social media advocacy as well as his blog, Hacking Christianity (HackingChristianity.net), featured on United Methodist news sources, National Public Radio, The Progressive Christian magazine, and Sojourners. Jeremy received the 2011 Young Alumnus Award from Boston University School of Theology for his blog and ministry.

Jeremy has degrees from Oklahoma City University (B.A. Religion) and Boston University School of Theology (M. Divinity). He and his partner Chelsea live with their three young daughters in the greater Seattle area.

Discussion Questions

Chapter 12:
To Reach the Nones and Dones,
Focus on the Ones
By Rev. Jeremy Smith

What does it mean to apply faith in a secular context?

Are there expectations for followers of your faith tradition? If so, what are they?

What are the benefits for people if they are involved in more than one aspect of church?

CHAPTER THIRTEEN

Connecting the Past and the Present

By Rev. Karen Yokota Love

He has shown you, O mortal, what is good.
And what does the Lord require of you?
To act justly and to love mercy
and to walk humbly[a] with your God.

– Micah 6:8 (NIV)[1]

My call into ministry is rooted in my context, culture, and my heritage as a Japanese American. I was formed and nurtured out of a Japanese American United Methodist Church in San Jose, California, located in one of the last three existing Japantowns in the United States of America, the other two located in San Francisco, and Los Angeles. I was baptized two months after being born, "a cradle Methodist," and grew up in the church. Vacation Bible School, Jr. High Camp, and Asian Camp were significant and recurring events that helped nurture and define my faith. It provided access to the multi-generational church that Wesley United Methodist Church is, while building relationships with my grandparents' friends, my parents' friends, and children younger than myself. I was involved in Church Family Camp, helped out at the Aki Matsuri, a Japanese Fall Festival, and danced in the San Jose Obon, a festival honoring the dead

---

1   Holy Bible, New International Version®, NIV® Copyright ©1973, 1978, 1984, 2011 by Biblica, Inc.® Used by permission. All rights reserved worldwide.

(think Dia de Los Muertos for Japanese people), which was hosted by the San Jose Buddhist Temple.

The United Methodist Church and the Buddhist Temple were the two main anchors in the San Jose Japantown. Our relationships were strong, and we collaborated frequently. A favorite memory of mine was watching the boys from the Buddhist Temple play basketball and going to their tournaments and dances. Many of us Methodist girls would go and mingle with the Buddhist people, and we all became friends. Living in a community with people of a different faith was a "normal" part of my church life. It was fluid and I realized that it helped nurture a sense of comfort as to not believing that Christianity was superior to other religions. It helped pave the way for future relationships with friends who are Muslim, Buddhist, and Jain.

Seventy-six years ago, Japanese Americans were imprisoned in concentration camps for two-and-half years by the United States government on the basis of racism and wartime hysteria. Here's the crazy part: my Dad was one of those prisoners. My father was born at Tule Lake Incarceration Camp, one of ten concentration camps where the Japanese American populations were forcibly confined during World War II. My mother was born and living in Hawaii at the time, where they were subject to a curfew. The majority of my relatives were forced into an incarceration camp, as they had no choice. Little did I know that this history would shape the rest of my life, as well as my call into ministry.

From the time that Japanese immigrants (*Issei*) started arriving in the late 1800s, they worked incredibly hard. Immigrant lifestyle was not easy. They were mostly low-income laborers and were banned from owning land or becoming citizens. The U.S. government halted immigration from Japan entirely in 1924.

The Immigration Act of 1924 limited the number of immigrants allowed entry into the United States through a national origins' quota. The quota provided immigration visas to two percent of the total number of people of each nationality in the United States as of the 1890 national census. It completely excluded immigrants from Asia. In 1917, the United States Congress enacted the first widely restrictive immigration law. The uncertainty generated over national security during World War I, made it possible for congress to pass this legislation, and it included several important provisions that paved the way for the 1924 Act. The first was a test that required immigrants over sixteen years old to demonstrate basic reading comprehension in any language. The second increased the tax paid by new immigrants upon arrival and allowed immigration officials to exercise more discretion in making decisions over whom to exclude. Finally, the Act excluded from entry anyone born in a geographically defined "Asiatic Barred Zone." (Under the Chinese Exclusion Act and the 1907 Gentleman's Agreement, Japanese and Chinese laborers were already excluded but Filipinos were exempt because the Philippines was a U.S. territory.) In all parts, the purpose of the 1924 Immigration Act was to preserve the ideal of American homogeneity.

Fast forward to 1941, when the Japanese government bombed Pearl Harbor. The U.S. government immediately arrested all Japanese American community leaders (our newspaper editors, our United Methodist pastors, Buddhist temples priests, etc.) and then, a few months later, issued that fateful order. Executive Order 9066 forced my family to give up their entire life —land, house, automobile, and freedom — to live in a desert prison camp. This was based on zero evidence of any Japanese Americans spying for the Japanese government.

My family's history led me to follow "my call" into ministry. My call is to serve and give voice to those who feel voiceless. I am driven to be an advocate and an ally to those who are experiencing similar hardships in today's context. When I arrived in the Pacific Northwest six years ago, I brought with me my passion for social justice work, and my desire to collect and tell stories. I was particularly interested in working with the Japanese American community to gather stories about the *Issei* (first generation of Japanese descent) and *Nisei* (second generation of Japanese descent) who were incarcerated, and to see how God works transformation through storytelling.

Storytelling, reframing, retelling, and sharing our experiences is cathartic and is a form of healing. In one of my first congregations, I worked with Whitney Memorial United Methodist Church, a Japanese American church that was humble in size. We told stories together and related the Gospel to their own stories and their own lives. Together, we collected stories, put them on paper, and worked to share their history and stories with the people in the community of Puyallup, WA. Puyallup is the very same location where some of these families were incarcerated seventy-six years ago at the Camp Harmony Assembly Center, (a euphemism used for a detention center) a place where the U.S. government kept Japanese American people prior to sending them away to the incarceration camps. Most of the prisoners who were at Camp Harmony were sent to either Minidoka Incarceration Camp in Twin Lakes, ID, or to Tule Lake Incarceration Camp in Tule Lake, CA.

I've found that through the sharing of stories and through education about the incarceration, there are new connections with the unchurched and people who identify themselves as "no religious affiliation." Since beginning my appointment at Mason United Methodist Church in Tacoma, Washington, I've been asked to present about the past, present, and future of the Japanese American people by speaking at the Day of Remembrance event at the University of Puget Sound, or giving walk-

126

ing tours of Tacoma's nearly vanished Japantown. Educating students, church members, friends, and community members is a critical part of my call.

For each church community that I've served, I've shared my story about the Japanese American experience. Last year, Mason United Methodist Church and an ecumenical cohort of pastors throughout the City of Tacoma affiliated with an organization called "Preaching Peace," helped to fold over 1,000 cranes for the Tacoma Day of Remembrance event at the Washington History Museum. We interacted with people from the City of Tacoma, from other churches, and other organizations in Tacoma to honor and learn about the forgotten Japanese American experience in Tacoma.

People in the Pacific Northwest are hungry for social justice work. They want to do good. Yes, we are in the None Zone where people are highly literate and organized religion isn't something that is a high priority or a part of the culture. But the work of justice isn't only for those who affiliate with a church. It's work that's beyond the church walls.

What Would Jesus Do? Jesus would want people to work together for the good, to treat and love our neighbor as we would like to be treated ourselves. We need to think about collaborating with outside organizations and non-profits to affect change at a larger level, rather than just within the church walls. I've discovered that people want to hear the story of my Japanese American heritage and my family's story, and they are curious about the history around it. They want to know more about how it relates to today's landscape and what we can do to make this world a better place. Millennials are driven by opportunities to provide community service, help people in need, invent new things, and generally make their mark on the world. Providing them with meaningful projects inspires them to work hard.

To be Christian doesn't mean we see Christ within the exclusive group of the church walls. To be a great Christian, and an effective Christian, means that we see Christ in everything, everywhere. We live out the Gospel and we model examples of how Jesus would've lived. We do the hard justice work, we get our hands and feet dirty, we walk in solidarity with the outsider, the oppressed.

As part of the justice work, last year, at Mason United Methodist Church, we heard a call and a cry from our students in the Proctor Tacoma neighborhood and around the entire country. An active lay member noticed that the March for Our Lives Tacoma group was searching for a meeting space, and suggested that they check with Mason.

March for Our Lives was a demonstration created and organized by #NeverAgain, a group of students who survived the February 14, 2018 shooting at Marjory Stoneman Douglas High School in Parkland Florida. The march not only remembered the seventeen students and faculty members that were killed that day, but it also served as a rally across America to say enough is enough to gun violence.

When I received the call I, along with our leadership team, was eager to open the doors to this group of young students. It was a good use of space for everyone: the Tacoma community, Mason United Methodist Church, and the local students. The students set up their headquarters at Mason. They organized themselves into different committees, each responsible for planning an aspect of the march. They discussed logistics and finances, they made signs, and planned the last details of the march. In addition to basic hospitality, members of our church provided snacks and pizza for the young organizers. This organized group of young people received a grant of $5,000 to offset costs of the March of Our Lives rally.

A seventh grader in Tacoma was the initial organizer of Tacoma's March for Our Lives. "I want to see something change," said the student. "I noticed things don't change unless somebody does something." Planning grew to include participants from all of Tacoma's public schools; student leaders representing high school and college students respectively.

Mason United Methodist Church youth members were an initial part of this organizing movement. Olivia shared that a recent phone threat at her school was very scary. She was participating because she didn't want to lose a friend or her sister to gun violence. "I want them to be safe," offered Olivia. Her sister, Ella, agreed adding, "I want to make a difference. With all of our young voices coming together, we can prevent a school shooting."

Mason United Methodist Church helped plant trees on "Green Tacoma Day," an annual day of service that offers great opportunities for the Tacoma community to get to know each other and our local green spaces. In conjunction with the City of Tacoma, in partnership with the Tacoma Public School district, we planted thirty-six trees around the perimeter of Mason Middle School which is directly across the street from the church. Mason served donuts and coffee to everyone in the community and it was in this space that we were able to introduce ourselves to the principal, teachers, and other community leaders of Tacoma. Mason supported the Tacoma School District during a two-week-long strike in the public school district. They also continue to be in relationship with the University of Puget Sound, which is within a two-block radius from the church. Christ's love is birthed through relationships within communities and neighborhoods, and healthy relationships are key.

Sharing stories and honoring the past, talking about the

present, and linking all of this to the future is vital to ministry. Being relational is key. The Japanese American experience not only revealed the endurance, perseverance, and
triumph of the community, it also exposed our nation's prob-
lem with racism and discrimination. As part of a group that
was detained and lost everything, confined to camps for years,
and then forced to rebuild a new life by starting from scratch,
it is our call to rise up and walk in solidarity with people who
are currently struggling.

We will never be free until all are free. Until the humanity
of African American people is affirmed and their safety and
freedom are secured, all people of color will still be second-
class citizens. Here's the real question, "What will we do in the
face of unprecedented direct attacks on others?" Will we join
the protests when ICE drags undocumented immigrants out
of their homes the way we were once dragged out of ours, or
will we stay silent? Will we support and advocate for Mexican
undocumented immigrants who are currently being separated
from their small children at the border and locked in detention
centers? Will we speak out against our country's deterioration
into a fascist regime feeding on the racism and xenophobia that
devastated our own community, or will we turn a blind eye?

It is a moment of truth for all of us. The moment calls for us
to reckon with the privilege we have and why we have it. And it
calls for each of us to look deep inside ourselves and ask what
comforts we are willing to sacrifice for freedom. It's a moment
to speak truth and love while living out the gospel, to treat our
neighbor, and to love our neighbor, as ourselves.

No one spoke up for the Japanese American community when Franklin Delano Roosevelt threw us into prison
camps. If we are silent when others are under attack, what
kind of justice is that? However, if we speak out, our support

will be powerful. Our potential, standing in solidarity in the movement for social justice is unlimited, and we are living out the gospel. Imagine the impact we could have.

In our churches, we are already equipped. We have the ability to fundraise, we can quickly bring people together, and we can utilize our professional talents and skills which are invaluable to the movement. We could take over the offices of elected officials after church every Sunday to demand sanctuary cities, train our Cub/Boy/Girl Scout troops and basketball teams in direct action, organizing against ICE, raise money for Black Lives Matter. The possibilities are endless.

The work of God is infectious, and God is working in Tacoma as well as the Pacific Northwest. Christ's transformative light enables us to do good to one another in an area where we are the least churched. Connecting people together and talking about the past in order to relate the past to the present is critical. Connecting different communities to new communities to work together is key. This, is loving our neighbor.

Reverend Karen Yokota Love serves as the pastor at Mason UMC and lives in Tacoma with her husband, Jesse. She has spent her life collecting stories about her ancestors' and community members' experiences to help bring to light justice and healing. Karen loves a good Netflix binge, getting her hands dirty in a creative D.I.Y. project, but also loves hitting a good yoga class, or taking long walks along Point Defiance in Tacoma. Yokota Love currently serves as a board member at the Tacoma Community House, a place that empowers immigrants and refugees to achieve their personal and professional goals. She's also an active member on the Pacific Northwest's Conference Commission on Race and Religion, and serves as the chair of the National Japanese American United Methodist Caucus.

Rev. Karen holds a Bachelor of Arts degree in Communications from the University of California, Berkeley, and a Master of Divinity degree from Claremont School of Theology in Claremont, California. Ordained as an Elder in 2018, she has served Milton UMC in Milton, WA, Whitney Memorial UMC in Puyallup, WA, and Puyallup UMC in Puyallup, WA.

Discussion Questions

Chapter 13:
Connecting the Past and the Present
By Rev. Karen Yokota Love

What issues of justice should the church be involved with?

Why is it important that a church be involved with teaching history to a community?

What does it take for a group to "walk with the outsider, the oppressed?"

A View From the Pew

By Lynne Pearson

I was raised in the United Church of Canada but found myself on the doorsteps of Bothell United Methodist Church in the fall of 1992. I wanted my daughter Joy to be baptized and my son Will was ready for Sunday school. It was important to my husband Matt and I that our children be raised in a faith tradition similar to our own. Many years later, I am still sitting in the pews at Bothell United Methodist Church. I embraced the United Methodist Church and it embraced me.

When Rev. Kristin Joyner and I first talked about putting this book together, I knew that God was at work in the Pacific Northwest. I did not know the creative ways in which United Methodist clergy and congregations were doing God's work. As each chapter of this book came in, my eyes were opened to the ways in which church has evolved in the None Zone. Congregations are being thoughtful about how they reach out. They are seeking to fill needs in communities, get messy, and try new things.

These clergy and congregations want church to be more than a Sunday morning experience. They want to make an impact both on the community level as well as the individual level. They are learning lessons along the way as they share God's grace and love.

From Rev. Kelly, I realized that it is not enough to just say, "Welcome!" When we want to invite someone in, we must first unlock the door. And prior to opening the doors, we may have to open our minds as well.

As I read Rev. Karen's chapter, I thought about the many populations that have been adversely affected by the actions of our government. The Japanese Americans were not the only people that were forcibly relocated. That is also the history of most Native Americans. Racism and hatred are fueled by ignorance and fear. When we truly interact with our neighbor, fear and ignorance are removed, and love has room to grow.

I am awed by Rev. Jenny's willingness to reveal so much of herself to her congregation. A painful experience for her was an opportunity for them to demonstrate acceptance and love. I am impressed with the far-reaching goals of her church. They intend to share God's love by planting new faith communities which may be new expressions of faith as well.

New expressions of faith are popping up around the area. There is a verse in a hymn that goes, "The church is not a building; the church is not a steeple; the church is not a resting place; the church is a people." By meeting in pubs Rev. Emma is providing a space for deep discussion, outside of a place that may make some people uncomfortable. I like this. I like that church does not have to be defined by walls.

Riverton Park United Methodist Church is putting up walls to help persons who are housing insecure in their area. Rev. Jan's church recognizes the value in everyone and has channeled its resources to reflect that recognition. They believe that in God's eyes we each have value and are deserving of dignity. It is not easy work that they do, and not every person helped is fully able to care for themselves independently, but the people they serve are filled with appreciation.

I was moved by the compassion extended by Rev. Heather and the church trustee. They didn't lecture the person who stole from them. They didn't preach to the person who stole from them. They forgave the person who stole from them, and then provided Christmas presents for his daughter. That was indeed a moment of grace.

Prior to reading Rev. Dave's chapter, I had never thought about Jesus as being disruptive. But, he was a thorn in the side of the Jewish leaders. He pushed back and challenged, which is what we are called to do when we see actions that go against God's call to love our neighbor.

There are those who believe that the church is no longer relevant and does not make a positive impact in today's world. However, the caregivers' group that formed in Rev. Meredith's congregation demonstrates the opposite. The caregivers shared their vulnerabilities, which allowed them to open up and receive the love and assistance the congregation was willing to offer. The caregivers, the care receivers, and the congregation were all blessed by this experience.

I don't believe that there is a benefit to living in isolation. I believe that gathering together makes us better people. I think that Rev. Joe's congregation is on the right track with the offering of small groups. Burdens are lessened when we share, more is accomplished when we work together, and we have the opportunity to be a blessing to each other. It is good to belong.

Reading about the Nones, the Dones, and the Ones, I questioned my own faith development. If my church experience was limited to only one thing, worship, or one activity, my relationship with God would be limited. I think, by asking congregants to be involved in one more thing, Rev. Jeremy is giving them an opportunity to deepen their faith.

Rev. Lara's congregation is very deliberate. Their purpose is to love, serve, and grow. Their purpose permeates how they view themselves as an organization and how they view themselves in their relationship with God. They are thoughtful and prayerful about what they do. They trust that God is leading them. Arising from that trust, the congregation is treating those around them with the respect, dignity, and love that God would want them to.

One of the best things a church can do is accept someone. Especially someone who does not fit societal norms of ethnicity, gender identity, physical ability, or social standing. Rev. Brad's church seeks to offer encouragement and acceptance. These can lead to community, which is something many people aren't aware that they are seeking themselves.

Community is at the heart of the work of Rev. Kristin. She sees the adverse effects that prosperity has brought to our region, families who are priced out of the housing market, homeless persons present where they never were before, and the need for affordable housing justice. Rev. Kristin works with cities and other faith groups to help the marginalized, to move them away from the margins and into the center. It is work that needs a partnership between faith communities, city governments, and citizens who are moved toward social action.

This is why the United Methodist Church is filling the void. It is not attempting to serve people where the church thinks they should be, but rather, is prayerfully and thoughtfully serving the people of the Pacific Northwest where they actually are.

Lynne Pearson

General Questions

Each author chose their bible passage for a reason. How does that chosen scripture guide their ministry?

How could you use a story as a guide in your community?

When have you shared your ministry stories with other churches and how did that affect the ministry?

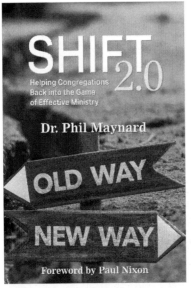
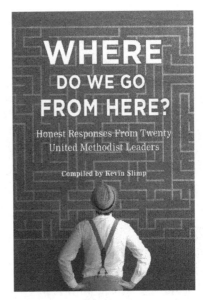

Grow Your Faith

with these books from Market Square

marketsquarebooks.com

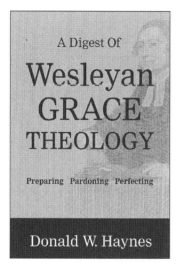

Wesleyan Grace Theology

Donald W. Haynes

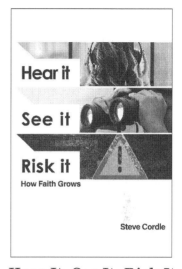

Hear It, See It, Risk It

Steve Cordle

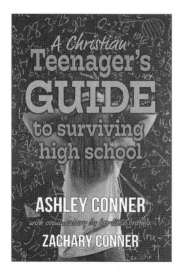

A Christian Teenager's Guide to Surviving High School

Ashley Conner

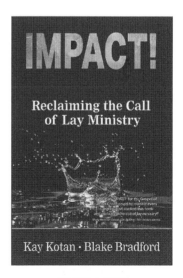

IMPACT!

Reclaiming the Call of Lay Ministry

Kay Kotan & Blake Bradford

Grow Your Church

with these books from Market Square

marketsquarebooks.com

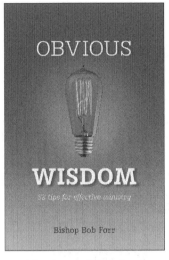

Obvious Wisdom

Bishop Bob Farr

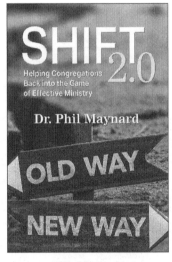

Shift 2.0

Phil Maynard

From Franchise
To Local Dive

Jason Moore & Rosario Picardo

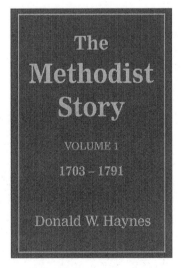

The Methodist Story
Volume 1: 1703-1791

Donald W. Haynes

38327945R00082

Made in the USA
San Bernardino, CA
09 June 2019